THE FIRST XV

*a selection of the
best rugby writing*

EDITED BY
Gareth Williams

PARTHIAN

Parthian, Cardigan SA43 1ED
www.parthianbooks.com
First published in 2011
This edition published 2015
© The Authors
ISBN 9781910901069
Introduction © Gareth Williams
Foreword © Gerald Davies
Cover design by Marc Jennings
Cover photo: photolibrarywales.com
Typeset by Elaine Sharples
Printed and bound by Gomer Press, Llandysul, Wales
Published with the financial support of the Welsh Books Council
British Library Cataloguing in Publication Data
A cataloguing record for this book is available from the British Library.

Contents

Editor's Introduction   i
Foreword   iii

HARRI WEBB
Vive le sport   1

W.J.TOWNSEND COLLINS
The master of supreme achievement   2

TERRY McLEAN
The greatest match of all   6

DYLAN THOMAS
Enoch Davies and a stranger   13

GWYN THOMAS
Padded up for action   16

ALAN WATKINS
Ups and downs of a climber   19

RICHARD BURTON
The last time I played rugby   22

JOHN MORGAN
Excursion train   30

DAI SMITH AND GARETH WILLIAMS
Cliff Morgan   34

JOHN REASON AND CARWYN JAMES
Gerald Davies and Barry John in New Zealand, 1971   39

GERALD DAVIES
Choking with Clive   46

FRANK KEATING
Phil Bach   52

EDDIE BUTLER
Prosser's Pontypool   58

RUPERT MOON WITH DAVID ROACH
Moonstruck   67

RICHARD DAVIES
Gone from under your nose   69

JOHN STUART WILLIAMS
River Walk, Cardiff   74

LEWIS DAVIES
Training night   76

ALUN RICHARDS
The flat on the Via I Monti   87

The Authors   97

Editor's Introduction

In 2007 I edited for the Library of Wales an anthology of Welsh sports writing called, unsurprisingly, *Sport*. The surprise to many lay in the quality of the writing it showcased; it has been twice reprinted. It offered a sporting smorgasbord – from bando to boxing and snooker to swimming (there was also some soccer) – varied enough to revitalise the most jaded palate, but maybe the meat came last, in the most substantial section which occupied almost a third of the entire book: 'Rugby'. This imbalance reflected not only my own sporting and literary interests but underlined the centrality in the popular and wider culture of Wales of what the late J.B.G.Thomas always referred to as 'the Game'. For over the years Welsh rugby has generated some classic writing, even if it has yet to attain the literary status enjoyed by cricket in England and boxing and baseball in the USA.

Parthian's Richard Davies is an award-winning writer and a former player. It's in his DNA. I was a spectator at the old Arms Park in the late sixties when his father Randall, the mildest person you could ever meet, was sent off during a notably bruising (i.e. dirty) game between Cardiff and Neath. With the nation gearing up for more bruising World Cup encounters in New Zealand, I accepted Richard's invitation to select a best fifteen from the forty odd pieces that appeared in the original *Sport* anthology. Here they are, with two new entrants that did not make the first cut, and two reserves. I wanted my 'First XV' propped by the poets who bookended the original selection, so a brace of bards, the one feisty the other wistful, find themselves on the bench. My selection has been shaped by the same principle as before: the best rugby writing is good writing that happens to be about rugby. Gerald Davies, who writes the Foreword, is as much an admirer of literary as of sporting elegance, and he has written on the game as stylishly as he played it. If I have needed an introduction, he needs none.

Gareth Williams

Foreword

I enjoy very much the crossing over of cultural boundaries. Of, say, a musician with whom we are familiar and recognise as the figure on the podium all dressed in black with a white dress shirt and a bow tie conducting the evening's music only for us later to notice him 'dressed down' with scarf and bobble cap among the madding crowd at Murrayfield. Or the elegant writer and broadcaster recording all of a nation's yesterdays and bringing that history to bear on today's events, and then to find him on the golfing greens of Augusta. Or the eloquent politician surviving the bear-pit confrontations of the House of Commons who, regretting the lack of respectful silence there, brings this rumbustious experience to his Saturday's outing by shouting away on the sporting terraces.

I find it somehow pleasing to find heroes from one way of life enjoying the thrills and fun of a different life; admiring and respecting the talent of others and entering the mood of the sporting spirit. These are people with a hinterland, not exclusively one dimensional, cherishing something beyond their narrow, though expert, field of endeavour. I am thrilled when such people say they love rugby, my passion.

The same goes for the solitary business of writing. Quite

simply I like it, having played rugby, to find that there are those who have the gift of translating the instant and instinctive action into words, creating a picture in the mind of what came and went in the blink of an eye and to understand why it happened and, perhaps, how it came to happen the way it did and thereby recording for all time the events of the day. Or the admiration the writer feels for a remarkable player who shapes an extraordinary event or a famous trip with a club gang and brings it all to memorable life.

In so doing they re-create the drama of what they saw and, more importantly, what they felt; of their encounter with the heroic, with mythical and lyrical embellishments of the pageant unfolding in front of them or, as Richard Burton writes, of 'the massive lies and stupendous exaggerations'. So long as it makes for a good read.

We warm to the adventure of the game from slow staccato beginnings to the final mad crescendo; or the other way round, of a game reduced to a longing for the referee's whistle to bring the whole dull, muddy rigmarole to an end and for an early beer to relieve the depression or to inspire a witty record of the slapstick event, 'Vive le Sport'; the mediocre which cannot be ignored but which frequently, by the stroke of a clever pen, can be transformed into enriching, guffawing comedy. There are the jokes and the ribald songs. There is the romance the writer senses. There is the high seriousness as well as the cheerfully peculiar which he reviews.

We will all conclude that in the larger scheme of things, sport is ultimately but trivial goings-on which we gladly embrace to relieve us of much that is ordinary and mundane, taking us out of the day's tedium to make us feel, or as close as it is possible to feel, that glad confident morning once more. Rugby, whether played at its glorious best or, for that matter, a simple unexpected and unadorned victory, uplifts us to make us feel better about ourselves and the world we inhabit.

Rugby can transport us into different realms. The game can either be painted in golden epic colours of international drama, in pastel shades of a casual rural scene, or sometimes, viewing the Pickwickian shape of the trundling tight-head prop, in bold and splashing tints of humour and even of farce.

Sport has the ability to do this and the writer is there to take us back to remind us of the exhilaration and the fun.

Gareth Williams' marvellous anthology gives us a wonderful taste of the kind of writing and the variety of styles that the game has inspired over the years. I wished for more. That he has included a piece of mine among the distinguished writers is an honour.

I hope the collection gives you as much pleasure as it did me.

Gerald Davies, CBE, DL

HARRI WEBB

Vive le sport

Sing a song of rugby,
Buttocks, booze and blood,
Thirty dirty ruffians
Brawling in the mud.

When the match is over,
They're at the bar in throngs,
If you think the game is filthy,
Then you should hear the songs.

from *The Green Desert* (1969)

W.J.TOWNSEND COLLINS

The master of supreme achievement

All my life through I have had a capacity for hero-worship. Whenever I have found greatness of character, intellect, skill, or kindliness it has been a joy to pay tribute to it. Yet, side by side with willingness to admire and praise (in connection with Rugby football and all else), has been an inability to ignore faults and shortcomings. In the early 'Nineties I thought Arthur Gould the greatest Rugby player I had ever seen. Today, after sixty years of football criticism, I think of him still as the greatest player of all time. There were days when he fell short of his own standards, and I criticised his play accordingly (much to the annoyance of some of his idolatrous admirers); yet, in spite of occasional defects, he seemed then, and to me remains, the master of supreme achievement. How wonderful were the days when Arthur Gould was the bright particular star of Invincible Newport and Invincible Wales! Under the heading of 'The Prince of Players', I wrote in 1893 or 1894 two articles which gave a full account of his career till that time. Its completeness was due to the fact that I had access to a newspaper cutting book in which Arthur Gould's admiring sister had kept records of most of the matches in which he had played. His career was remarkable in its variety. Though Newport was his home, and early and late he played for the Newport team, he spent long periods in other districts, part of the time associated with a brother who was a public works contractor. He played for the Southampton Trojans, the London Welsh, and Richmond; for Hampshire, South Wales, and Middlesex; from 1885 till 1897 he was assured of his place in the Welsh team, of which he was the accepted captain for years. Those who never saw him in his heyday can have little conception of his physical powers and the keen brain which directed and controlled them. He was a track sprinter only two yards outside evens; and a great hurdler who several times was second in the English championship. As a footballer he had all the gifts, and they had been developed by thought and constant practice. Some boys when they begin to play Rugby football find that they dodge, swerve, and side-step naturally – it is not a question of thought, it is an animal instinct. Arthur Gould was one of them. He dodged or swerved away from a tackler instinctively; but before he had gone far he had learned to study the capacity of his fellow players and the defensive powers of his opponents, knew what he was doing, why he did it, and how it was done. Other players, on their inspired days, have gone through their opponents – swerving, side-stepping, dodging with easy mastery which made the defence look silly; other centres have made perfect openings and unselfishly given their wings chances to score; other men have nipped their opponents' attacks in the bud by the quickness with which they smothered man and ball, or by intercepting passes; others have tackled man after man or compelled them to pass to avoid being taken with the ball; but no three-quarter I have known has maintained the high level of attainment in attack and defence so long and so consistently as Arthur Gould – no man has shown such uniform brilliance and resourcefulness over so long a period of years. He was in first-class football from 1882 till 1898; he first played for Wales against England in 1885, and his last game was against England – at Newport in 1897 – twenty-seven matches, at that time a record. And when comparison is made with the records of other players it must be remembered that in his day there were no matches with France, New Zealand, South Africa, or Australia to swell the record, and that he was in the West Indies in 1889. As a boy he played at three-quarter, but it was as a stop-gap full-back that he entered the Newport XV. His first game was prophetic. 'Kick, you young devil!' shouted the Newport Captain, for he was playing a three-quarter game; but twice he ran through the Weston-super-Mare team and scored tries. As a full-back he played for Newport for three seasons; he got his cap for Wales first as a full-back; but when he had a chance to play at three-quarter he soon made his mark. In those early days he was famous as a kicker, and one season dropped twenty goals; but he was known also for his speed and elusiveness, and for the wonderful quickness of his punting. Thereby hangs a tale. Arthur Gould was left-handed and left-footed; he kicked instinctively with his left foot. But when his opponents found that he could kick only with one foot, they played on him from their right and smothered his kicks. When he found what was happening, he practised kicking with his right foot so assiduously that he became as good with one foot as the other, and the late W.H.Gwynn, of Swansea, Secretary to the Welsh Rugby Union, who told the tale, concluded, 'And you simply couldn't prevent him from getting in his kick.' Never did a rugby player work harder to improve his natural gifts and perfect his technical equipment. As time went on, he became sparing of his efforts to drop goals, and concentrated upon running through the defence or making openings for his wings. In his closing years his defence was criticised, and it is true that often in those late days he would not go down to the ball, and obviously avoided clashes with big forwards who were bearing down on him; while too often he tried to intercept a pass instead of going for the man with the ball. This of course was a defect – it counts against him. But he had taken a lot of battering, and had suffered many injuries in the earlier years, when his defence was the admiration of friend and foe. Indeed, after the Welsh victory over Scotland at Newport in 1887-8, Charles Reid, the greatest of Scottish forwards, said publicly that he had never known a man who did more for his team than Gould did that day. When Gould ran, he carried the ball in both hands; often as he side-stepped an opponent he raised the ball at arm's length above his head; sometimes from that height he gave a downward untakeable pass. I mention faults developed late in his career, because if they are ignored I may be charged with praising this great player blindly or dishonestly. But, when all is said, Arthur Gould is to me the greatest rugby footballer who ever played.

from *Rugby Recollections* (1948)

TERRY McLEAN

The greatest match of all

And so the game began. Straightway was remarked a strange lethargy about the All Black movements. Because they had travelled so much and understood each other so well, the New Zealanders glossed over their mistakes with a kind of professional competence. But there were mistakes, all the same, and alone among the teams of the Kingdom the Welsh had the wit to perceive and the knowledge to employ the means of capitalising them. So often in the past the ball had flashed from the scrum into the hands of Roberts and gone from him in smooth movement to Stead, to Hunter at the start of a weaving run and thence into the three-quarters and sometimes back to where Seeling and O'Sullivan and McDonald and Glasgow hunted and hungered like black panthers. Now, there were awkward movements, fumblings, slow passes and aimless runs which drifted across the field into touch. Time and again Gillett hefted the ball and, more often than not, it swerved into midfield so that All Black heads rolled and began to hang as they chased hither and thither.

Where Gillett aimed and misfired, Winfield, steady as a rock, planted the ball unerringly ahead of his forwards into touch.

Where Mynott stumbled outward, Percy Bush nipped and jigged. And while the All Black forwards for the main part had the advantage, this was slight. Wales had deduced that the New Zealand formation of seven forwards, seven backs and Gallaher as half one and half the other was more elastic and hence more dangerous than the standard formation of eight forwards and seven backs, and with that imitation which is the sincerest form of flattery they had made their Cliff Pritchard a rover, too. His roving here and there was the ruin of a number of attacks at their inception; and when he was beaten on the tackle, the Welsh backs, all enduring, thudded into their markers and put them down as comprehensively as if the Leaning Tower itself had bitten the dust of Pisa.

So the play went for half an hour. As someone afterwards remarked, keen, strenuous and intensely exciting, yes. Brilliant, no. Then Wales breached the New Zealand 25 and heeled from a scrum somewhat to the right of the posts. It was the moment to execute the planned attack. Owen feinted to the right, to the blindside, and in the confusion seemed to run a yard or two wide of the scrum. The All Black defence bore across, rapidly massing. In a moment, Owen flung back a pass to Pritchard to the left of the scrum. Away went Wales. Now Gabe in the centre had the ball and was thrusting ahead. As a tackler loomed he passed onward to Morgan on the left wing. Years later, Morgan's mind seemed to grow clouded on issues of the game and a famous statement of his on events was taken as gospel truth – as it might have been – and made thousands of New Zealanders embittered. At this moment, all that mattered was the present and in it Morgan was at the height of manhood and dangerously quick in his running. Clasping the ball, he sped around the lumbering stretch of Gillett and flew a few yards onwards for a try. Forty thousand Welshmen screamed their delight. Teddy! Teddy! Did you see it, man, did you see him get the ball and go! Lord, what a run! And did you see Gabe, man, and Cliff Pritchard? And Owen, Dicky Owen. He fooled 'em. Dicky fooled those bloody All Blacks, man.

Winfield could not manage to goal, but it was Wales 3 and New Zealand 0 and so it remained at half-time which, proclaimed two minutes too soon, caught the New Zealanders storming at the Welsh goal-line and battering down the defence, too. Now was seen the almost professional competence of the All Blacks. Though Bush once caused swelling screams of joy and hope as his dropkick soared toward – and only just dropped short of – the posts, the attack was principally delivered by New Zealand. The old, smooth, rippling movement of men and ball toward the goal-line wanted in rhythm and fluency, but its substitute, an honest, almost tormented endeavour, seemed too strong for Wales. McGregor once placed the ball back in mid-field from the centre and, with a surer grasp, anyone of half a dozen forwards could have had the ball and a try. Another time Roberts snapped the ball to Mynott with the goal-line only feet away; but Welsh hands turned Mynott for the time being into the Leaning Tower of Taranaki and struggle as he might he could not score.

And then came the moment which was to stand not only this match but all of Rugby on its ear, not for a spell but for generations, which was to engender a feeling that New Zealand had been unfairly used and which, when all the pros and cons had been argued into eternity, was to be the greatest event in the history of New Zealand Rugby because it provided a basis, a starting-point, a seed of nationalism upon which all aspects of the game were to depend in succeeding years. Wallace the Nonpareil dashed in and, gathering the ball, set off from near halfway, bearing to his left and weaving and swerving away from the tiring mass of Welsh players. Nothing that this genius ever did on the field was marred by gross miscalculation or foolish blunder and now, with the light in his eye and the honour of New Zealand to save, his flying run shouted of death and destruction, no matter how much Wales might or could endure.

Striding up to join him ran young Deans, the powerful centre, and as they rushed onward in concert the youth sensed that Wallace might be covered. He called and the pass came swiftly to him as he thundered for the goal. He dived –

And then, of course, all hell let loose.

Gabe tackled Deans. It was certain that they lay a moment. It was also certain that soon Welsh reinforcements were pulling the two back into the field and not wasting any time about it, either.

The question was whether Deans had grounded the ball across the tryline, or not. Gabe felt that he had not, because he could feel Deans straining forward as they lay on the ground. Wallace and other New Zealanders swore that he had. The Welshmen, of course, were far too busy. Never were traces of a crime – and, in Wales, it is a crime to score against Wales – so swiftly expunged.

And the only man in all the world whose yea or nay meant anything at all was, poor fellow, in a state of utter confusion. Poor Mr Dallas, a Scotsman, had taken the field as referee heavily clad and without bars to his boots. He was not in fine training. The pace of the game was great. At this vital moment when all he needed to do was to be there and to see for himself, giving a judgment which all would have to respect, he was not present. Like a blunt-nosed trawler shipping steep seas, he was trudging along a good 30 yards behind the play.

When he did get up, Deans and Gabe lay in the field. The Welsh expungers had been diligent at their task. Mr Dallas blew his whistle; but it was not for a try.

You may, if you wish, even now embroil yourself in the aftermath. Gabe has stated that he said to Deans, after the game, 'Why did you try to wriggle onward?' There was no reply. There is evidence that Gallaher had no complaint. But the next day, at 10.26 a.m., Deans handed in to the Cardiff Post Office a telegram to the London *Daily Mail*. 'Grounded ball six inches over line,' he wrote in it. 'Some of Welsh players admit try. Hunter and Glasgow can confirm was pulled back by Welshmen before referee arrived.'

Deans was a man of complete probity. It was unthinkable that he would deliberately falsify the issue. And, years later, the issue was bedevilled still further when Morgan, now Dr Morgan, wrote on a programme that it was a try. Fifty years later, those few, those gallant few, who remained of this incomparable team were treated to a reunion by the New Zealand Rugby Union and, as is the custom, gathered in a hotel bar to drink and talk. It was a moving experience to hear Hunter say to Stead, while the years peeled off their shoulders back to the days when they were stalwart and strong and without compare, 'Without you, I should have been nothing. You were the finest player of all.' But it was also wryly moving that the gathering had scarcely got going before Wallace was producing a diagram which purported to show where he had run, when he had passed, and how Deans had scored. The old men grouped about it. 'Yes,' they said. 'That is right. That was how it happened. It was a try.' In all this seriousness, there is a touch of the comic, if not irreverent, in the evidence of George Nicholson, an Auckland forward who had not won a place in the match. 'Billy Stead,' Nicholson said, 'was touch judge. Bill felt the call of Nature. He asked me to take over. When Wallace began to run, I went with him. I was only yards away when Deans got the ball. I was whooping along. And then I saw the dive and the tackle.'

'And what was it?'

'Ah,' said George. 'It was a try, true enough.'

So it can go and has gone on. And yet, what did it matter? What does it matter? Only one man in all the world could decide and he said no. That was the end. The place of the 1905 All Blacks in history is secure. No other team ever approached their back play. By modern standards, Seeling and McDonald and Casey and O'Sullivan and the rest were small forwards; but so powerful were they, so husky, so well trained, so tough, that for all time they fulfilled Falstaff's dictum that it is the spirit and not the size of the man that counts.

It is fascinating, if fruitless, to speculate on the might- have-beens if the try had been awarded and Wallace, as he would almost certainly have done, had kicked the goal. Would Rugby in New Zealand have remained the national game? Would the rivalry with Wales still be of a special quality which none but New Zealanders and Welshmen can ever properly understand? One speculates and gets no further. Was it a try? Of course not. The referee said so.

Fifty years later – and in fifty years you can cover most of the arguments – Stead said, almost as if he were ruminating, 'We did not deserve to win. Wales had the better team on the day.' When wisdom speaks, let all other tongues be silent.

New Zealand: G.A.Gillett (Canterbury), D.McGregor (Wellington), R.G.Deans (Canterbury), W.J.Wallace (Wellington), J.Hunter (Taranaki), S.J.Mynott (Taranaki), F. Roberts (Wellington), D.Gallaher (Auckland), captain; A.McDonald (Otago), C.Seeling (Auckland), J.J.O'Sullivan (Taranaki),

F.Newton (Canterbury), F.T.Glasgow (Taranaki), G.Tyler (Auckland), S.Casey (Otago).

Wales: H.B.Winfield, W.Llewellyn, Gwyn Nicholls (captain), R.T.Gabe, E.T.Morgan; Cliff Pritchard (extra back); P.F.Bush, R.M.Owen; W.Joseph, C.Pritchard, A.F. Harding, J.F.Williams, G.Travers, J.Hodges, D.Jones.

Referee: Mr J. D. Dallas (Scotland).

The day was fine, but the pitch was heavy. The attendance was 40,000. Wales scored 23 minutes after the start. This was the 28th match played by the All Blacks in three months.

Footnote: The discussion over the 'Deans' try became an international affair to which every Welshman desired to be a party. It has been calculated, from the vehemence of their arguments and the apparent sincerity of their statements, that some 2,000,000 Welshmen were present at Cardiff Arms Park at the time. One writer even claimed to be sitting within six yards of the spot where Deans was grounded.

Many years later, Seeling and G. W. Smith, who after the tour both played Rugby League in Lancashire, were taken on the turf of Cardiff Arms Park. Seeling dug his umbrella into the turf and with tears streaming down his face said, 'This was the spot.' (But it was Seeling who, not long after the tour, exclaimed that the All Blacks had lost because 'they done their nuts.')

The 1953 All Black team streamed on the field at its first visit to Cardiff and a local guide headed purposefully for a corner. 'Here it is,' he exclaimed. He dug his heel into the turf. 'Away out here?' said an All Black wonderingly. 'Golly, not even Billy Wallace could have kicked the goal from here.' 'No, no,' said the Welshman. 'This was where Morgan scored.'

from *Great Days in New Zealand Rugby* (1956)

DYLAN THOMAS

Enoch Davies and a stranger

The Blue Bull, the Dragon, the Star of Wales, the Twll in the Wall, the Sour Grapes, the Shepherd's Arms, the Bells of Aberdovey: I had nothing to do in the whole, wild August world but remember the names where the outing stopped and keep an eye on the charabanc. And whenever it passed a public-house, Mr Weazley would cough like a billygoat and cry, 'Stop the bus, I'm dying of breath!' And back we would all have to go.

Closing time meant nothing to the members of that outing. Behind locked doors, they hymned and rumpused all the beautiful afternoon. And, when a policeman entered the Druid's Tap by the back door, and found them all choral with beer, 'Sssh!' said Noah Bowen, 'the pub is shut.'

'Where do you come from?' he said in his buttoned, blue voice. They told him.

'I got an auntie there,' the policeman said. And very soon he was singing 'Asleep in the Deep'.

Off we drove again at last, the charabanc bouncing with tenors and flagons, and came to a river that rushed along among willows.

'Water!' they shouted. 'Porthcawl!' sang my uncle.

'Where's the donkeys?' said Mr Weazley.

And out they lurched, to paddle and whoop in the cool, white, winding water. Mr Franklyn, trying to polka on the slippery stones, fell in twice. 'Nothing is simple,' he said with dignity as he oozed up the bank.

'It's cold,' they cried. 'It's lovely!'

'It's smooth as a moth's nose!'

'It's better than Porthcawl!'

And dusk came down warm and gentle on thirty wild, wet, pickled, splashing men without a care in the world at the end of the world in the west of Wales. And, 'Who goes there?' called Will Sentry to a wild duck flying.

They stopped at the Hermit's Nest for a rum to keep out the cold. 'I played for Aberavon in 1898,' said a stranger to Enoch Davies.

'Liar,' said Enoch Davies.

'I can show you photos,' said the stranger. 'Forged,' said Enoch Davies.

'And I'll show you my cap at home.'

'Stolen.'

'I got friends to prove it,' the stranger said in a fury. 'Bribed,' said Enoch Davies.

On the way home, through the simmering moon-splashed dark, old O.Jones began to cook his supper on a primus stove in the middle of the charabanc. Mr Weazley coughed himself blue in the smoke. 'Stop the bus,' he cried, 'I'm dying of breath!' We all climbed down into the moonlight. There was not a public-house in sight. So they carried out the remaining cases, and the primus stove, and old O.Jones himself, and took them into a field, and sat down in a circle in the field and drank and sang while old O.Jones cooked sausage and mash and the moon flew above us. And there I drifted to sleep against my uncle's mountainous waistcoat, and, as I slept, 'Who goes there?' called out Will Sentry to the flying moon.

from 'A Story' in *A Prospect of the Sea* (1955)

GWYN THOMAS

Padded up for action

I've just emerged with a torn pelt from a furious faction fight between supporters of rugby on the one hand and soccer on the other. Until that meeting I had no idea of what it would feel like to emerge at speed from a burning kraal. Now I think I know.

Rugby, as played by the Welsh, is not a game. It is a tribal mystery. This fancy for violent movement, for suddenly scragging a fellow human who is trying to pass you, probably goes back far into time. It might have been a device to fool the Normans into thinking that we were constantly mobilising for another round of playing it up around Chepstow.

If the place had been flat, it would not have been so bad, but time and again, in the deeper valleys, teams have played on pitches with a slope of one in three, where they take their half-time slice of lemon in an oxygen tent, and have rubber barricades at the bottom of the ramp against which players and referee can be bounced back into play when they go hurtling down with their brakes burned out.

Strategic use was often made of these conditions. A visiting team would turn up at the changing room on a Saturday afternoon. The changing room was almost invariably a pub. Hospitality would be lavish.

A tidal wave of ale would hit the new arrivals, laced on high occasions with meat pies like cannon-balls. Then beer-logged and replete, the visitors would be led to the field. The road could well be a thousand feet of up-winding goat track, and committee men would course like corgis on the flanks of the convoy, keeping the glassy-eyed gladiators on course.

Up on the plateau, the referee would go around making sure that the players were facing in the right direction. When the massive bodies met in direct assault you could hear the glug two valleys away. When the fire of battle had been stoked to a maximum, and the referee had been crushed out of sight in a marshier section of the pitch, the committee would then nip in and remove the ball to save wear and tear.

Back in the pub there would be a specially darkened room for the handing back of limbs.

My own experience as a young rugby player was brief and rugged. My impulses as a sportsman were not dynamic. I did a little with a game called 'catty and dog', played by beating a short stick sharply with a long stick. I also made occasional appearances as a very casual cricketer, emerging as a bowler with a special line in balls that went in and off the gas-works container that overshadowed our minute pitch. I also went in for a simple version of quoits played with stones and later taken over by a rockery tycoon.

But at grammar school I was singled out by a Rugby Union dervish who had soccer and cricket tabbed in the same category as yaws. He had seen me once in spectacular flight from a wild dog. It was about my only burst of speed. Normally I move very slowly except when frightened at the prospect of rabies. The master told me that with my type of springy, bandy leg I could develop a body swerve that would fox even Interpol.

He foxed me. The school pitch was a kind of gravel and coke dump. If you took a series of falls (and the sensible ones took just one fall and then stayed down, groaning and quietly burrowing out of sight into the coke) you got up looking like a fuel briquette, and spent the following lesson winkling bits of coke out of the skin.

The field ended, on the school side, in a sharply sloping bank. Whenever I broke into a run I seemed to be within inches of this slope. As soon as I got the ball, the master would urge me loudly to use my natural body swerve. I would disappear over the bank, and genuinely glad of the trip.

There was only one player on the field more inept than myself. He was a monster of about 15 stone, who spent most of his time standing stock still in a corner, turning his head slowly and trying to figure the whole thing out.

One day when I was coming down the field at some speed, galvanised this time not by a rabid hound but by the coach – who was barking in a way that would have had Pasteur worried – I rammed the monster. He didn't budge. I went flat. And then, quite solemnly and without malice, he boarded me as if I were a bus. Honourably injured, I was allowed to go back to quoits and corrupting indolence.

The incident left me with nothing worse than a curious psychosomatic limp, which I am still able to summon when wishing to deepen perplexity or to explain my distrust of strenuous sport.

from *A Hatful of Humours* (1965)

ALAN WATKINS

Ups and downs of a climber

This week I propose to write the brief life of a rugby player, R.H.Lloyd-Davies. He came from my native village, Tycroes, Carmarthenshire, and was seven years older than I was. His full name was Rheinallt Lloyd Hughes Davies, but he was known locally as Hugh Lloyd Davies. The initials and the hyphen came later, for Hugh, despite his many outstanding qualities, was a bit of a climber. His family owned one of the two bus companies operating from the village, Tycroes being particularly well-endowed with this form of enterprise. Though the family were prosperous, they were not ostentatious or grand. His father worked as a conductor on the family buses to give himself an occupation.

Hugh, along with his brother and sister, attended the Amman Valley County (subsequently Grammar) School, Ammanford. When he went up to Cambridge later, and was asked where he had been at school, he would reply: 'Amm*a*nford, actually', placing the accent on the second syllable. A peculiarity of his childhood was that he was brought up by his grandparents, who lived just down the road, while his siblings remained with his parents. Anyway, it was said that Hugh was spoiled. He was, however, denied a bicycle. He was told that, as he could travel free on the buses at any time he liked, he did not need a bicycle.

As a sixth-former he had an affair with the French mistress. This was prosecuted vigorously during bouts of fire-watching, a duty which teachers and senior pupils were required to undertake. They married when he was in his early twenties. Hugh had always enjoyed (or suffered from) a sexual drive well above the average. Like most successful practitioners in this field, he was both bold and undiscriminating. He was also handsome, with pale, smooth skin, black curly hair that grew in a peak, very bright eyes and very white teeth. He possessed loads of charm. In drink, however, he could turn verbally vicious.

He was a fast, adventurous full-back, and a schoolboy international. From school he was conscripted into the RAF, where he soon became a pilot officer. He played in the great inter-service and representative matches at St Helen's, Swansea, and for Wales, first against New Zealand, the 1945 Kiwis, and then against England in the 1946 Victory International. In neither match were his experiences particularly happy. Against New Zealand he kicked the ball straight at J.R.Sherratt, who promptly scored. Against England another wing, R.H.Guest, evaded him to score two tries. Hugh resented the non-award of caps for this match, and kept claiming – what was morally true but factually incorrect – that he was a Welsh International. However, he confidently expected to be in the post-war side. But the selectors preferred Frank Trott of Cardiff, less spectacular but much safer.

From the RAF, Hugh went up to Trinity Hall, Cambridge, to read law. He won the university match of 1947 by kicking two penalties, six points to Oxford's nil. On the morning of the game he had been roused from a deep slumber by two friends, given a shower, dressed and poured on to the team coach. Shortly afterwards he was sent down from the university. He was in a pub, a proctor arrived, and ordered him to leave. The proctor, Trevor Thomas, was not only a law don at Hugh's college but came from Swansea. Hugh addressed him familiarly in Welsh, telling him not to be so silly. Thomas was not amused.

Nevertheless he joined Gray's Inn and played for London Welsh and Harlequins, where, he said, you met a better class of girl. Finding himself short of money, he joined Barrow – the first Cambridge Blue to go north. He was paid a thousand pounds, played a couple of matches and then promptly decamped to Paris.

Returning to London, he had several encounters with the law, culminating in a nine months' prison sentence for attempting to pawn stolen jewellery. During the early 1950s, he was in Tycroes, doing odd labouring jobs. He then went back to London. There were reports of sightings. He was passing himself off as a colonel; had gone bald; was sleeping rough; was a gardener with the Islington council. A few months ago, I was told that he had died last year.

from *The Independent* 23 October (1987)

RICHARD BURTON

The last time I played rugby

It's difficult for me to know where to start with rugby. I come from a fanatically rugby-conscious Welsh miner's family. I know so much about it, have read so much about it, have heard with delight so many massive lies and stupendous exaggerations about it, and have contributed my own fair share, and five of my six brothers played it, one with some distinction, and I mean I even knew a Welsh woman from Taibach who before a home match at Aberavon would drop goals from around forty yards with either foot to entertain the crowd, and her name, I remember, was Annie Mort and she wore sturdy shoes, the kind one reads about in books as 'sensible', though the recipient of a kick from one of Annie's shoes would have been not so much sensible as insensible, and I even knew a chap called Five-Cush Cannon who won the sixth replay of a cup final (the previous five encounters, having ended with the scores 0-0, 0-0, 0-0, 0-0, 0-0 including extra time) by throwing the ball over the bar from a scrum ten yards out in a deep fog and claiming a dropped goal. And getting it. What's more I knew people like a one-armed inside-half – he'd lost an arm in the First World War –

who played with murderous brilliance for Cwmavon for years when I was a boy. He was particularly adept, this one, at stopping a forward bursting through from the line-out with a shattering iron-hard thrust from his stump as he pulled him on to it with the other. He also used the misplaced sympathy of innocent visiting players who didn't go at him with the same delivery as they would against a two-armed man as a ploy to lure them on to concussion and other organic damage. They learned quickly, or were told after the match when they had recovered sufficiently from Jimmy's ministrations to be able to understand the spoken word, that going easy on Jimmy- One-Arm was first cousin to stepping into a grave and waiting for the shovels to start. A great many people who played unwarily against Jimmy died unexpectedly in their early forties. They were lowered solemnly into the grave to the slow version of 'Sospan Fach'. They say that the conductor at these affairs was noticeably one-armed but that could be exaggeration again.

As I said, it's difficult for me to know the end. The last shall be first, as it is said, so I'll tell you about the last match I ever played in.

I had played the game representatively from the age of ten until those who employed me in my profession, which is that of an actor, insisted that I was a bad insurance risk against certain dread teams in dead-end valleys who would have little respect, no respect, or outright disrespect for what I was pleased to call my face. What if I were unfortunate enough to be on the deck in the middle of a loose maul... they murmured in dollar accents? Since my face was already internationally known and since I was paid, perhaps overpaid, vast sums of money for its ravaged presentation they, the money men, expressed a desire to keep it that way. Apart from wanting to preserve my natural beauty, it would affect continuity they said, if my nose was straight on Friday in the medium shot and was bent towards my left ear on Monday for the close-up. Millions of panting fans from Tokyo to Tonmawr would be puzzled, they said. So to this day there is a clause in my contracts that forbids me from flying my own plane, skiing and playing the game of rugby football, the inference being that it would be all right to wrestle with a Bengal tiger five thousand miles away, but not to play against, shall we say, Pontypool at home. I decided that they had some valid arguments after my last game.

It was played against a village whose name is known only to its inhabitants and crippled masochists drooling quietly in kitchen corners, a mining village with all the natural beauty of the valleys of the moon, and just as welcoming, with a team composed almost entirely of colliers. I hadn't played for four or five years but was fairly fit, I thought, and the opposition was bottom of the third class and reasonably beatable. Except, of course, on their home ground. I should have thought of that. I should have called to mind that this was the kind of team where, towards the end of the match, you kept your bus ticking over near the touchline in case you won and had to run for your life.

I wasn't particularly nervous before the match until, though I was disguised with a skull-cap and everyone had been sworn to secrecy, I heard a voice from the other team asking '*Le ma'r blydi film star 'ma?*' (Where's the bloody film star here?) as we were running on to the field. My cover, as they say in spy stories, was already blown and trouble was to be my shadow (there was none from the sun since there was no sun – it was said in fact that the sun hadn't shone there since 1929) and the end of my career the shadow of my shadow for the next eighty minutes or so. It was a mistaken game for me to play. I survived it with nothing broken except my spirit, the attitude of the opposition being unquestionably summed up in simple words like 'Never mind the bloody ball, where's the bloody actor?' Words easily understood by all.

Among other things I was playing Hamlet at that time at the Old Vic but for the next few performances after that match I was compelled to play him as if he were Richard the Third. The punishment I took had been innocently compounded by a paragraph in a book of reminiscence by Bleddyn Williams with whom I had played on and off (mostly off) in the RAF. On page thirty-seven of that volume Mr Williams is kind enough to suggest that I had distinct possibilities as a player were it not for the lure of tinsel and paint and money and fame and so on. Incidentally, one of the curious phenomena of my library is that when you take out Bleddyn's autobiography from the shelves it automatically opens at the very page mentioned above. Friends have often remarked on this and wondered afresh at the wizardry of the Welsh. It is in fact the only notice I have ever kept.

Anyway, this little snippet from the great Bleddyn's book was widely publicized and some years later by the time I played that last game had entered into the uncertain realms of folk legend and was deeply embedded in the subconscious of the sub-Welshmen I submitted myself to that cruel afternoon. They weren't playing with chips on their shoulders, they were simply sceptical about page thirty-seven.

I didn't realize that I was there to prove anything until too late. And I couldn't. And didn't. I mean, prove anything. And I'm still a bit testy about it. Though I was working like a dog at the Vic playing Hamlet, Coriolanus, Caliban, The Bastard in 'King John', and Toby Belch, it wasn't the right kind of

25

training for these great knotted gnarled things from the burning bowels of the earth. In my teens I had lived precariously on the lip of first-class rugby by virtue of knowing every trick in the canon, evil and otherwise, by being a bad loser, but chiefly, and perhaps only, because I was very nippy off the mark. I was 5ft 10½ ins in height in bare feet and weighed, soaking wet, no more than 12½ stone, and since I played in the pack, usually at open side wing-forward, and since I played against genuinely big men, it therefore followed that I had to be galvanically quick to move from inertia. When faced with bigger and faster forwards, I was doomed. R.T.Evans of Newport, Wales and the Universe for instance – a racy 14½ stone and 6ft 1½ ins in height – was a nightmare to play against and shaming to play with, both of which agonies I suffered a lot, mostly thank God, the latter lesser *cauchemar*. Genuine class of course doesn't need size though sometimes I forgot this. Once I played rather condescendingly against a Cambridge college and noted that my opposite number seemed to be shorter than I was and in rugby togs looked like a schoolboy compared with Ike Owen, Bob Evans or W.I.D.Elliot. However, this blond stripling gave me a terrible time. He was faster and harder and wordlessly ruthless, and it was no consolation to find out his name afterwards because it meant nothing at the time. He has forgotten me but I haven't forgotten him. This anonymity was called Steele-Bodger and a more onomatopoeic name for its owner would be hard to find. He was, I promise you, steel and he did, I give you my word, bodger. Say his name through clenched teeth and you'll see what I mean. I am very glad to say that I have never seen him since except from the safety of the stands.

In this match, this last match played against troglodytes,

burned to the bone by the fury of their work, bow-legged and embittered because they weren't playing for or hadn't played for and would never play for Cardiff or Swansea or Neath or Aberavon, men who smiled seldom and when they did it was like scalpels, trained to the last ounce by slashing and hacking away neurotically at the frightened coal face for 7½ hours a day, stalactitic, tree-rooted, carved out of granite by a rough and ready sledge hammer and clinker, against these hard volumes of which I was the soft-cover paper-back edition. I discovered some truths very soon. I discovered just after the first scrum, for instance, that it was time I ran for the bus and not for their outside-half. He had red hair, a blue-white face and no chin. Standing up straight his hands were loosely on a level with his calves and when the ball and I arrived exultantly together at his stock-still body, a perfect set-up you would say, and when I realized that I was supine and he was lazily kicking the ball into touch, I realized that I had forgotten that trying to intimidate a feller like that was like trying to cow a mandrill, and that he had all the graceful willowy-give and sapling-bend of stressed concrete.

That was only the outside-half.

From then on I was elbowed, gouged, dug, planted, raked, hoed, kicked a great deal, sandwiched, and once humiliatingly taken from behind with nobody in front of me when I had nothing to do but run fifteen yards to score. Once, coming down from going up for the ball in a line-out, the other wing-forward – a veteran of at least fifty with grey hair – chose to go up as I was coming down if you'll forgive this tautological syntax. Then I was down and he was up and to insult the injury he generously helped me up from being down and pushed me in a shambling run towards my own try-line with a blood-curdling endearment in the Welsh tongue, since during all these preceding ups and downs his unthinkable team had scored and my presence was necessary behind the posts as they were about to attempt the conversion.

I knew almost at once and appallingly that the speed, such as it had been, had ended and only the memory lingered on, and that tackling Olivia De Havilland and Lana Turner and Claire Bloom was not quite the same thing as tackling those Wills and Dais, those Twms and Dicks.

The thing to do, I told myself with desperate cunning, was to keep alive, and the way to do that was to keep out of the way. This is generally possible to do when you know you're out-classed, without everybody knowing, but in this case it wasn't possible to do because everybody was very knowing indeed. Sometimes in a lament for my lost youth (I was about twenty-eight) I roughed it up as well as I could but it is discouraging to put the violent elbow into the tempting rib when your prescience tells you that what is about to be broken is not the titillating rib but your pusillanimous pathetic elbow. After being gardened, mown and rolled a little more, I gave that up, asked the Captain of our team if he didn't think it would be a better idea to hide me deeper in the pack. I had often, I reminded him, played right prop, my neck was strong and my right arm had held its own with most. He gave me a long look, a trifle pitying perhaps, but orders were given and in I went to the maelstrom and now the real suffering began. Their prop with whom I was to share cheek and jowl for the next eternity, didn't believe in razor blades since he grew them on his chin and shaved me thoroughly for the rest of the game, taking most of my skin in the process, delicacy not being his strong point. He used his prodigious left arm to paralyse mine and pull my head within an inch or two of the earth, then rolled my head around his, first taking my ear between his fore-finger and thumb, humming 'Rock of Ages' under his breath. By the end of the game my face was as red as the setting sun and the same shape. Sometimes, to vary the thing a bit, he rolled his head on what little neck he had around, under and around again my helpless head. I stuck it out because there was nothing else to do, which is why on Monday night in the Waterloo Road I played the Dane looking like a Swede with my head permanently on one side and my right arm in an imaginary sling intermittently crooked and cramped with occasional severe shakes and involuntary shivers as of one with palsy. I suppose to the connoisseurs of Hamlets it was a departure from your traditional Prince but it wasn't strictly what the actor playing the part had in mind. A melancholy Dane he was though. Melancholy he most certainly was.

from *Touchdown* (1970)

JOHN MORGAN

Excursion train

The rain eased last night five minutes before the excursion train to Scotland for the Welsh Rugby match was due out of Swansea. The men who had been pretending they were waiting for the rain to ease ran from the ex-international's pub across the station yard swinging their flagons or carrying their crates like soldiers rushing ammunition to the guns. In the hallway an undergraduate stood holding a bunch of delicately wrapped leeks, looking very much like a man waiting for his mistress in a sensitive British film, but not talking like one. He had lost his ticket.

After a man had rushed through our crowded Pullman car shouting 'Moses, Moses, where are you Moses?' we settled down quietly for the twelve-hour journey through the night. Young men played cards for fun. In another car a frail middle-aged man with his false teeth on the table in front of him joined in singing 'I Believe', obviously not knowing the words. When 'Calon Lân' began he put his teeth back in his mouth. In the mixed car – the girls being of most ages – there was some shouting and a *bonhomie* so humid that, transmuted, it trickled down the window panes.

Two men, both over seventy years of age, at my table, after establishing that they had a mutual acquaintance of preachers and minor bards, began a recondite philological discussion in Welsh. The man in the grey suit and brilliant white collar, his face scrubbed until it shone had postulated this argument: some Englishmen and some renegades say that Welsh is a dead language because it borrows from the English. Well then, what about telephone? 'What about telephone indeed,' said his new friend, the man in the navy blue suit and striped flannel shirt.

'Telephone is from the Greek.' 'Those Greeks were a brilliant lot.' 'What is the English for telephone?' 'Ask you may.'

'Telephone!'

While they considered this point the man in the white collar offered me a Minto and his friend offered a Cymro Mint. I accepted both and offered a swig from my flagon. 'Strict T.T.,' they said.

'There is no 'th' in the Welsh alphabet,' said the white-collared man.

'You are quite right,' said the other.

'In Ireland they spell the word telephone with an 'f'. Now then.'

I left them to their discussion and their bags of sweets and moved down the train where men were arranged to sleep in remarkable postures. I settled myself down as some town passed by in the darkness and the rain. A stranger offered me a Scotch to drink and talked about opera until he suddenly fell asleep when explaining to me the plot of Don Giovanni. Sometime around five o'clock the familiar cry of a Welsh woman calling her friend sounded through the compartment. Marie was the friend's name. The sound was more like a cockerel crowing in a quiet valley at dawn than anything else.

A young man was pounding the table and shouting, 'I'll

31

never leave Wales again.' He had been ill all through the night. At another table a freshly shaved man was drinking beer out of a pint pot, eating last night's sandwiches, and reading about Formosa. The lady found her friend; the boy gave up pounding; the car became very quiet.

What does a man do when he arrives on a bitterly cold winter's morning in Edinburgh before dawn? He trails, hot sand in his eyes, in the train of tradition. He hands his bag through the luggage hatch and helps two solemn-faced jokers to lift their crate of Guinness into the same place. He then walks up Princes Street to Scott's Memorial, warms at a brazier, turns about and walks back in the dawn to a restaurant that opens at seven.

'Would you find this in Swansea? Would you find this in Cardiff?' demands a Welshman gone native. He has been here before and knows about this restaurant and is proud of that.

A man eats two breakfasts and reads what the native experts have to say about the match. He notes that the Scots have taken to trusting in miracles.

It is then time to gawk at the Firth of Forth bridge, be restored by the first breezes and to ride back through the countryside into a city awake and alive with Welshmen. We join up with compatriots who have been in Edinburgh two or three days, and walk the streets and the shops staring at everything and listening to the people who actually speak with a Scotch accent as they do in the films.

Most of us have either scarlet berets or scarlet and white scarves, or leeks or daffodils. Some have all these things and also carry saucepans. Everyone is tremendously polite and cheerful. Even the rain stops and the sun shines. People in the know tell us that we must be at Murrayfield by two o'clock if we want a good view of Scotland being trodden into her own turf. And while, of course, we all feel sorry for poor Scotland, we don't feel all that sorry. 'Have a good journey up?' asks a man selling views of the Castle. 'Quiet,' says a customer.

'A very quiet journey, but God help us to-night if we win,' he pauses. 'Or especially if we lose.'

from *The Observer* 5 February (1955)

DAI SMITH AND GARETH WILLIAMS
Cliff Morgan

The succession [in 1951] of William Benjamin Cleaver by
Clifford Isaac Morgan as Triple Crown fly-half confirmed a
long-held suspicion that, years ago, one of the lost tribes of
Israel had somehow wandered into South Wales. Cliff always
played with the passionate urgency of a man trying to get out
again. With the ball held at arm's length in front of him, his
tongue out almost as far, his bow legs pumping like pistons,
eyes rolling, nostrils flaring, and a range of facial expressions
seldom seen north of Milan – either at the opera house or the
soccer stadium – the dark-haired, Celtically-constructed,
perky Morgan was, at 5ft 7ins and 12 stone, the identikit
Welsh outside-half. But no-one could have assembled Cliff; he
was an amalgam of the social and cultural forces that had
shaped modern Wales and of the currents that were defining
Welshness anew in the second half of the twentieth century.
Cliff came from Trebanog, a precipitous offshoot of the
Rhondda, on whose windy ridge people clung together for
warmth and safety lest the storms of the world blew them
away; he would never lose a sense of this induced Welsh,
almost cosy, togetherness. His was the Welshness of a

34

nonconformist home where Mam ruled and Sunday was for chapel, which meant that Cliff was humming snatches of oratorio before he was out of the shawl. The rugby crowds of the 1950s – strong, now, on 'Calon Lân', 'I Bob Un', 'We'll Keep a Welcome', and 'The Holy City' ('... lift up your gates, and sing') – were the last of the harmonious generations brought up on choir practice and the Band of Hope. If there had been room on the terraces to dance then the incessant rain of the fifties would have completed a mass Welsh imitation of the era's favourite Hollywood musical; and if that international crowd could have managed something from the Messiah – as, in the fifties, sections of it still could – the chorus best calculated to inspire Cliff Morgan would have been 'Let us break their bonds asunder'. It might have been written with him specifically in mind – South Wales is liberally endowed with Handels – for Cliff's india-rubber face typified the unbelievable springiness of his whole body: a favourite ruse of his for evading the clutches of opponents who had managed actually to lay hands on him was to go limp in their embrace; then, as the tackler momentarily relaxed his grip, Cliff jumped out of the tackle with an agility that made Harry Houdini look arthritic, and scurried away.

Born in 1930, Cliff had gone to Tonyrefail G.S. and came under the sensitive care of sportsmaster E.R.Gribble. It was 'Ned' Gribble who in 1956 would lead a W.S.S.R.U. party – with Alan Rees (Glanafan G.S.) and Clive Rowlands (Ystradgynlais G.S.) at half-back – to South Africa, where it won seven of its eight matches. His reputation as a rugby mentor was established by his nurturing of the effervescent genius of the boy Morgan, whom he guided to international schoolboy honours just after the war. It was not only the joys of rugby that Cliff discovered in school, but his own Welsh identity. Writing on the occasion of the Urdd Jubilee Match (Gêm y Dathlu), played, to celebrate the fiftieth anniversary of its founding, at the National Ground in April 1972, where both teams were selected by two other former Urdd members and international fly-halves, Carwyn James and Barry John – it was 'The King's' last appearance and he left as a lingering memory a ghostly fifty-yard solo try – Cliff Morgan recalled what Urdd Gobaith Cymru (the Welsh League of Youth) had done for him. 'It was around the age of eleven or twelve that I became a member of the Urdd at Tonyrefail Grammar School. D.J.Williams ran a flourishing branch with a variety of activities. Visits by Dr Iorwerth Peate, the doyen of Folk Life Studies, Cliff Jones, the Welsh rugby international, a trio from University College, Cardiff, and a Folk Group from Pontlottyn. We had dances and discussions, Noson Lawen and Mabolgampau [sports]. But it wasn't until I went to the Urdd camp at Llangrannog about 1945 or 6 that I really felt a sense of Welshness and of belonging. It's easy to fall in love with Llangrannog with its beaches and the green-blue sea...' Cliff had fallen in love with a Welshness that was, culturally and geographically, distinct from the one he knew in his native Rhondda. His reinforced sense of identity reflected a muted national awareness of broken links that rumbled off-stage during the 1950s. Lacking the sharp edges, the readiness to defy authority and challenge power structures that became features of Welsh political and language movements in the sixties and seventies, the mini-nationalism of the fifties – the Parliament for Wales movement led by Lady Megan Lloyd George, ex-Liberal and Labour M.P. for Carmarthen from 1957 to 1966, and S.O.Davies, Labour and then Independent Labour M.P. for Merthyr from 1934 to 1972; the Welsh Schools movement that made inroads into anglicized Glamorgan (though, as late as 1951, most Welsh speakers still lived there); the campaign for the formal recognition of Cardiff as Wales's capital city – was most agreeably personified on the rugby field by Cliff Morgan.

His international career – he played his first home game for Cardiff at nineteen against Oxford University in October 1949 – extended from the drawn match with Ireland in 1951 to the historic 16-6 defeat by France at Cardiff in 1958. During the course of his twenty-nine-cap career he adjusted his play to the changing requirements of those years. By instinct an attacking player of unquenchable spirit, he played his finest running game for Wales in 1952 against Ireland. His most memorable Welsh try was also against Ireland in 1955 when a generally lifeless game was transformed in its last quarter when Wales suddenly ran up 18 points in as many minutes to turn a 3-3 stalemate into a 21-3 demolition job. The points avalanche included one furiously individualistic try by the Trebanog terrier as he tore into a thicket of defenders, got lost, and shot out the other side and over the line. But there was more to his game than just pyrotechnics. Though sometimes as unpredictable as a jackie-jumper, he generally jumped with a purpose. He spent his whole rugby career working endlessly for an extra half yard of space; when he failed to pierce the defence himself, his pass often did, and he gave a masterly exposition of his skill as distributor, as well as dodger, in partnership with England's Jeff Butterfield in South Africa in 1955, when his pass in itself often put that gifted centre into the gap.

From that year on, he revealed extra qualities as tactical kicker and tireless coverer. In 1958, his creativity increasingly at the mercy of tighter back-row defences and ruthless midfield marking, he harnessed the notorious Twickenham swirl and dominated the match tactically to earn an injury-hit Wales a 3-all draw by kicking cleverly and insistently to the right-hand corner in the lee of the west stand. Beneath the lilting voice and warm personality there was a decisive streak that later took him to the Head of BBC Outside Broadcasting. In the scarlet jersey he learned decisiveness the hard way. Against Ireland, on his debut, he faced Jack Kyle. He was rightly apprehensive of the Irishman's reputation, but as the game progressed and Kyle seemed reluctant to do anything much, Morgan allowed his attention to flicker. Kyle sensed it and was suddenly past him for a crucial, equalising score...

from *Fields of Praise* (1980)

JOHN REASON AND CARWYN JAMES

Gerald Davies and Barry John in New Zealand, 1971

The Lions had to make use of any ball that New Zealand kicked away. They had to develop the counter-attack and they had to develop the confidence to use it under pressure. The All Blacks and the provincial teams had a tendency to overkick when trying to hoist the ball into the box behind the forwards on the blindside wing, and so the Lions' wings had to stand deep so that they were in effect playing as three full-backs. Then they could support each other in their counter-attacks. This had its greatest moment in the match against Hawke's Bay when J.P.R.Williams caught a narrowly missed kick at goal behind his own posts and launched a surging counter-attack, which ended with Gerald Davies scoring a try between the posts at the other end of the field. Davies was then in the blazingly high summer of his powers, and in the match against Hawke's Bay, he gave such a comprehensive demonstration of the range of his skill that it was as if the Fates had decreed that he should be given one chance to compress the magic of his career into one afternoon.

He took that chance by scoring four tries, three of them as a wing and one of them in his old position as a centre. All were exquisite examples of the most beautiful of the running skills.

For the first five years of his career, Gerald Davies had played as a centre. It was from that position that he scored the most memorable try of the Lions' 1968 tour of South Africa. This was in the Lions' match against Boland, in the Cape Province, and running with the ball from a line-out in his own half, Davies saw that the opposing outside centre had come up too fast in defence. This meant that the Boland defensive line was dog-legged, and Davies made a searing break on the outside before twice sidestepping the cover and running on for seventy yards to score.

Strangely enough, the final try that Davies scored against Hawke's Bay in 1971 was very similar. He had moved into the centre after an injury to Mike Gibson, and when Duncan, in the Hawke's Bay centre, came up too fast in defence from a scrum near his 25, Davies streaked past MacRae on the outside and side-stepped the full-back to score by the posts.

By that stage of Gerald Davies' career, centre-three- quarter play had become much more physical and as he was small and lightly-built, he had accepted advice to move out to the right wing. Initially, he was rather reluctant to accept this advice, because he felt he would see much less of the ball. Towards the end of his career, his fears in this respect were fully justified, but at that time, John Dawes was playing in the centre in the Welsh team and he was such an unselfish player and such a supreme passer of the ball that Gerald Davies was persuaded that there was a whole new world waiting to be conquered on the wing.

The way he conquered that world was one of the supreme satisfactions to be had from watching British Rugby in those few fleeting years when it was at its zenith. Thomas Gerald Reames Davies met all Dave Gallaher's exacting requirements as a back. He had scalding pace and breath- taking acceleration and he had the rare gift of being able to side-step at pace off both feet. Bleddyn Williams insists that very few players have ever been gifted with a true side-step, which is the ability to execute the manoeuvre without perceptible loss of pace, but Gerald Davies was unquestionably one of them.

Being so lightly built, Davies had to develop the instincts of the forest animal. He knew his body was fragile, so he had to depend on speed and alertness and quickness of thought and footwork. Fear is an important element in the make-up of such a player, just as it is in that of the forest animal. It heightens perception, and the adrenalin secreted adds to the surge of acceleration.

Gerald Davies also played the game with his head. He was aware of the possibilities offered by variation in the length of his stride. He learned what paid and what did not pay and he remembered. He learned to stay out in defence and mark his man and to leave the inside man for the cover. He could read the game because he had acute footballing intelligence. His positional work and his assessment of the possibilities of counter-attack were excellent. He was a killing runner-in of tries and yet he knew when he was not going to score and invariably contrived to make the ball available for his support. Mick Molloy, who played in the second row of the pack for Ireland for many years, once said ruefully that he had lost count of the number of games he had played at club and national level in which his own team and all its aspirations had been dashed by one devastating run by Gerald Davies. Wales made nothing like the use of him towards the end of his career that his talents demanded, and for that his

41

opponents all over the world were eternally grateful, but he was that rarity in any sport, a player whom all his rivals acknowledged as the master.

Carwyn James treasured him, as he did all his other gifted backs, but he knew that if those gifted backs were to have the chance to express their skills, the Lions' forwards would have to come to terms with the realities of rescuing every scrap of possession, often from a position of weakness. He knew that on many occasions, the Lions would not be rucking in the ideal situation of going forward. Frequently, they would have to ruck or maul in retreat, and so it was important that they should know how to do it and that they should practise it regularly. That practice alone paid dividends in the first test, when the All Blacks were so much the better side, and yet the Lions got away with a victory.

Finally, the Lions were helped by the fact that there were players in the team who had been to New Zealand and who knew what it was all about. Gareth Edwards and Barry John had toured New Zealand in 1969 and had been rated as non-entities. Their coach was delighted. He knew that two years later, Edwards and John would want to prove themselves, and they did. By the seventh match, when the team played quite beautifully and destroyed Wellington, the Lions felt that they were capable of a genuine roar. Even the brutal match against Canterbury a fortnight later, in which they lost their two test props for the rest of the tour because of injury, did something for the Lions. In one way it was a disaster, the low point of the tour, but after darkness there has to be light, and that match made the Lions more determined than ever to prevail. 'We shall overcome,' they sang. And they did.

... The impact in Britain of the achievements of the 1971 Lions surprised even the players. The phlegmatic British sporting community came as near as it ever will to a ticker-tape welcome, and in Wales, at any rate, the returning heroes went back to their villages in motorcades.

The focal point of this adulation was Barry John, who not only broke the scoring record for a tourist in New Zealand, but practically doubled it. Typically, he sensed the type of welcome that would be waiting if he went back to Wales by an orthodox route, so he slipped home unobtrusively and went to ground. Again, no one laid a finger on him.

This was one of the most extraordinary features of his play. He did not have either the scalding pace or the startling acceleration which is almost indispensable to a back, but his running had a ghost-like quality which made him infinitely elusive. He achieved this partly by variation of pace and by the variation of the length of his stride and partly by mesmeric use of the ball, or his hips, or his shoulders, or his feet. One New Zealand flanker confessed ruefully, 'Barry John rolled his eyes, and I fell over'.

Barry John was not a classical passer of the ball, but in the words of Mike Gibson, one of his greatest admirers, 'He got it there'. Barry John also had staggering self-confidence and he was a merciless exploiter of individual weaknesses in the opposition. He was a beautiful kicker, too, and he was left-sided in so many activities that he kicked very well off his left foot. He was fragile in build, and so, like Gerald Davies, he had the same awareness of physical danger as a forest animal. Perhaps this helped him to find as much time and as much space as he did. Certainly he had the rare gift of being almost able to transcend the game in which he was playing and to regard the opposition almost with pity. He had one of Lewis Jones' qualities, too. He could go from third gear to top and then into overdrive and he would surprise an opponent each time. He did it with much less use of energy than Lewis Jones, and he sensed the relative balance of an opponent like that of a dancing partner.

He sometimes did unexpected things in defence. He originated the gentle self-derision about his 'finger-tip tackling,' and yet he once stopped Benoit Dauga, the great French lock, five yards from the line at the cost of a broken nose. This saved an international match for Wales against France. In the first test in New Zealand in 1971, he found himself confronted with Colin Meads snorting round the end of a line-out only twenty yards from the Lions' line. The Lions could not go to his assistance and all Barry John could do was get in Colin Meads' way, but he did that, inelegantly but effectively, until help arrived.

He was completely unaware of the organisational technique of Rugby football. He just was not interested. 'Just give me the ball,' he said. He would go to sleep in the team talks when Clive Rowlands was coach of Wales. He got on like a house on fire with the massive intellect of Ray McLoughlin, and every morning tried to remember whether McLoughlin was a loose head donkey or a tight head donkey, but when McLoughlin shared a room with him on tour, and asked him to specify what he would do in certain match situations so that the forwards would know in advance in which direction to run, Barry John asked, his eyes round with wonder, 'How can I tell you? I don't know myself until I get the ball'.

Barry John created his own private world in the dressing room before a match. He shut himself within himself. He did not want a build-up. He created a personal privacy which was so complete that no coach ever thought of intruding. Other players need attention, or reassurance, or motivation. Not Barry John. The only organisation that interested him was soccer. In many ways, he was a much greater student of soccer than rugby. He knew the strengths of soccer players and could have been a professional himself. He would have enjoyed that. He would have taken to big time soccer like a duck to water.

... He commanded a game from the kick-off. 'Let's see the numbers on their backs first,' he would say. 'Let's see them going backwards.' He could also destroy any opponent who was one-sided, as he did his rivals at outside-half in Wales, and he scored tries with such a complete lack of fuss that opponents rarely touched him. He was the first Rugby player in Britain to be crowned. The Lions called him 'The King'. In Wales, he was all but deified as well, but in the end, he gave it all away, and he did it almost off-handedly.

He played for one more season after the 1971 tour and then retired. He had been crowned the 'King' not only of Welsh Rugby, but of British Rugby too, and it was probably the larger public which felt the keener disappointment at his departure. That public sensed, just as Gareth Edwards sensed, that John and Edwards were on the threshold of a new dimension of half-back play. From Britain's point of view, even more than from the Welsh point of view, it would have been absorbing to see what more they could achieve.

from *The World of Rugby* (1979)

GERALD DAVIES

Choking with Clive

There's a knock at the door. J.P.R. gets up slowly, opens it and immediately falls back into bed, hardly checking on the person who wants to come in. He peers, bleary-eyed, at his watch. Nine o'clock. Nine-o'-blasted-clock.

'Good morning, boys,' chirps Gerry, sauntering gaily in. He has already started his relatively early morning round. 'Both all right? Sleep well?'

'Apart from the noise of the traffic, a couple of fire brigades and forgetting to turn off the central heating – apart from that OK,' I mumble from under my blankets.

'It's only nine o'clock, Gerry. Have a heart!' pleads J.P.R. He asks for some physiotherapy later on, then his head hits the pillow again.

'Yes, yes, of course. Weather's fine, it'll be a running game today,' says Gerry cheerily, hardly noticing our complaints. He has become accustomed to them over his years with the team and will encounter similar moans in other rooms on a match day. He details the morning timetable: '11.30 team talk, Room 320. Lunch at 12, OK?'

Muffled noises from the two beds. Out goes Gerry to

complete his round, keeping everyone informed and treating the needy, especially the sensitive, 'piano-playing' backs. The routine has begun.

Left alone, we turn uneasily in our beds. We try to grab some more rest, but it's a futile hope. We both know that the day has started and it's going to be a long morning. Best, though, to keep away from the milling crowds downstairs in the hotel foyer, and bed is as good a place to be as any.

The telephone rings.

'There are supposed to be no calls before eleven. Didn't you tell the receptionist?' grumbles J.P.R.

'I thought you did that.'

I pick up the receiver. 'Is that you, Del?' enquires the anonymous and out-of-breath voice at the other end.

'No, wrong room.'

The voice is not deterred. It asks: ''Aven't got any tickets by any chance, 'ave you?'

'No!'

Down goes the receiver. It is the first of many such calls. At this point let's turn the clock back, back to an Edinburgh hotel room during Clive Rowlands' reign as coach. That was when the success began, and when Clive brought his own flavour and fervour to pre-match tean talks. At 11.25 on the morning of the match, the room would be gradually filling as the players arrive. Some are earnest-looking, some joking. Most look untidy, their flowery shirts lack the matching ties and are open to the chest. But Shadow – Dai Morris to the Bob Bank crowd – who was up early and who, alone, has dared venture into town, is immaculate in a clean yellow shirt and carefully knotted Barbarians tie.

There's plenty of colourful talk, too: staccato sentences from the nervous new members, relaxed and light-hearted conversation and banter among the experienced. Out of the hubbub one voice (from the front-row union, of course) rises above the rest to enquire of Gareth Edwards about the health of the 'King', Barry John, and to ask what it is like to share a room with him. The 'King', Gareth reports, is shaving. The front-row union express mock surprise that the 'King' is performing this humble task himself: 'Can't quite be royalty yet, then.'

'You wait,' says Gareth, quick as a flash, 'you wait till he cuts himself – the blood comes out blue orright!'

John 'Mr Greedy' Lloyd comes in and asks for his mate Shadow. 'Sign these,' he says. 'They're for the boys at school.' He passes over some autograph books, miniature footballs and a motley collection of hotel paper and menus to be circulated among the players.

The room is now nearly full, both of smoke (although only Clive Rowlands has a cigarette) and of bodies. Both beds are in danger of collapsing; one of them supports the weight of five forwards, as well as Phil Bennett, a reserve today, huddling uncomfortably between the mighty shoulders of his fellow sospans, Del Thomas and Barry Llewellyn. The other players are lying all over the floor.

'Everybody here, then?' says Clive. 'Good. On time too.' Somebody corrects him – one player is missing.

'Where's John Bevan? Not still in bed is he? Keith, go and get him. Tell him to hurry – a minute to go.' Clive parades up and down what little space there is left in the room, puffing at his cigarette.

Ray Williams, the coaching organiser, walks in and is reminded that he is only just in time. Dapper he is, in a lightweight suit. 'New suit, Ray?' someone shouts from the overloaded bed.

'Yes. Smart, eh?'

'Very nice. Pity they didn't have it in your size though.' Everybody laughs.

'Cheeky!"

John Bevan rushes in and apologises to Clive.

'You're lucky,' says Clive. 'You had two seconds to spare, else it would've been fifty press-ups.' No one is sure whether he is joking. 'Orright. Turn the radio off. Out here, Gareth. Let's have a shout. Let's get a proper frame of mind.'

Out comes Gareth to the front, to the tiny space, to simulate the call for the first scrum. 'On the call then, boys …together…ready… steady, Jeff. Ball in…*now*!' And there's a chorus of noise.

'Not good enough,' insists Clive. 'Do it again.'

'Hold it, Jeff. Ball in…*now*!' And again the chorus, backs and forwards alike, shouting to raise the roof.

'Better, better. Once more,' says the familiar gruff voice. The accumulated cigarette ash droops. Once more Gareth coaxes the imaginary first scrum. 'Great, great,' comes the reward from Clive. 'Now we're together.' And there is seriousness and total silence in the cramped room as the ash from his cigarette falls and disintegrates on the floor. Clive begins to talk.

'This match is important. It's important that we win and win well. We haven't come all this way to lose. Think' – there's nothing else to do in that room now – 'think of your families at home, of your friends who've travelled up to see you play. And not only to see you play, but to see you win. For Wales. Do you know', he says, 'do you know what I saw in the hotel foyer just now?'

We are listening intently for the little anecdote that he unfailingly provides, either quoting a misguided pressman to make us angry, or giving an example of some people demonstrating their unashamed patriotism to make us even more emotional, to make the ticker tick that little bit faster. 'There they were,' he goes on ''alf a dozen of them, walking into the hotel, one of them with a telly under his arm. Imagine it, a TV – "Just in case we don't get a ticket, see, Clive." You may think it funny, but that's enthusiasm for you boys. They're all there behind you, willing you on to win. Fifteen thousand of them have travelled all the way up here to see Wales win. For those at home in Cefneithin, there's no stop-tap this afternoon. And if you win there's an extension till five tomorrow morning.'

Silence. Phil, bunched between Llew and Del, smiles at this. The King smiles too, but no more than that.

'Now come on.' Clive drags out those last two words. 'We haven't travelled all this way for nothing. No fear. We've come to beat them, and in their own territory. We're the best in Europe. We've proved it. And we're going to prove it again this year. We're going to win. What are we going to do, Jeff?'

'Win,' comes the reply, almost apologetically. 'What?' asks Clive, aggressively.

'Win.' A little louder this time, but still half-heartedly. 'Can't hear you. What did you say?' Goading him this time.

'WIN!' he bellows. They must hear it in Cefneithin. 'That's better. Let's hear it next time. It's going to be hard.'

We've got to take the game to them, we mustn't let them get on top. That first ten minutes is vital. Vital. They're going to come at us like bats out of hell. So in the scrums and line-outs we must have tight control. Go down in the scrums together, all eight, tight. Right, Jeff? No penalties, no nonsense. Right?'

And on he goes, his emotive voice brandishing words like

an old-time evangelist, picking on individual players: Gareth to have good ball, Barry to control it, Arthur Lewis to tackle, tackle, tackle: wings get back, help in defence to start the counter. Oh, we've got to win, we must win. For our friends, for our country – for Wales.

It's vital, vital. My ticker is going like the clappers. He thumps his chest with the cigarette-free hand. 'We've got to win. We must win.' The sweat is running down his face.

'What are we going to do, John? What are we gooing to do, Mr Greedy? Eh?'

'Win.'

'Yes, yes. And if your opposite number gets anywhere near you, what will you do? What will you do?

'I'll...' he stutters, 'I'll...I'll eat him!'

Silence. Phil is the first to giggle, then Barry, then Jeff and finally the whole room erupts with laughter. Clive, leaning forward, hands on his knees, is choking himself.

Mr Greedy looks incredulous and insists, 'I will beat him. Wales will beat them all.'

from *Gerald Davies, An Autobiography* (1979)

FRANK KEATING

Phil Bach

For a slight man, Bennett had astonishing power with his right-footed kicking from the ground but, particularly, with his punts. I can close my eyes now and see that great swingeing follow-through of his – standing upright, but his right boot finishing higher than his Celtic-black smear of hair, like the very best downstage hoofer at the Paris Folies. He was from Felinfoel, a nondescript scrabble of a large village which brews the watery beer of the same name, and just down the high hill from Barry's Cefneithin on the road which drops on into Llanelli. The choice was 'coal or steel'. Phil's father chose the steelworks – the 'Klondike', they called it. His mother worked at the local car-pressing plant. He was a sickly child, pasty-faced and off-sick and inevitably with a snivelly nose. But mad about sports. And a week's bright-red asterisk was Saturday when Dad, back from his night-shift labours in the furnaces, would have three boiled eggs for breakfast, take off his hobnails and overalls, bath, have a cat-nap... then, refreshed and glad at heart, walk the boy down to Stradey, to The Match. Hand in hand on the 'tanner bank' where, Uncle Thomas-John alongside, they would watch the Scarlets play.

One day, when the boy was nine, they took him down to St Helen's for the crunching death-or-glory annual against Swansea, and many years later, in a marvellously touching memoir he wrote with Martyn Williams, Phil recalled:

'The platform at Llanelli General was a sea of red caps, scarves, mufflers and cloth caps. It was a massive pilgrimage, which had left villages and homes deserted of menfolk. St Helen's, I thought, could never accommodate this moving mass of miners, steelworkers, teachers, ministers and boys. They were all good-humoured; the bantering, the jokes, the bets, everything adding to the excitement of the afternoon.

'It was a Derby spectacular, hard, rough and uncompromising. Skirmishes on the field started fights on the terraces; the shouting and the noise was incredible and I kept tight hold of my father's jacket. Swansea were leading by 5-3 in the second half, with precious few minutes to go before the end. Suddenly Carwyn James at outside-half made a half-break and passed to his centre Denis Evans, who gave the ball to Geoff Howells and by that time there was sufficient room for Geoff to round his man in the corner and race for a try underneath the posts. St Helen's went mad! Hats, programmes, bags and newspapers were flung into the air. Some five thousand Llanelli supporters had witnessed one of those Scarlet miracles.'

The fly-half who had manufactured that winning try for Llanelli was, of course, Carwyn James. If the tot Bennett was nine, it must have been 1958, the year Carwyn was capped for Wales.

So it was fifteen winters later, early in 1973, on a still, and ever will be, celebrated afternoon at Cardiff Arms Park that the names Bennett and James came together in tandem for world consumption (although, by then, Wales – certainly West Wales – knew the pairing of the coach James and the springheeled little fly-half had for some seasons lit dazzling flares for the club at Stradey Park).

Bennett had at once assumed John's mantle for Wales and played in the defeat by New Zealand at the start of the 1972–3 season and in the first match of the Five Nations, when England were well beaten. Bennett's performances in both games did not receive widespread acclamation. Compared to the man he succeeded, Phil was frankly a visible worrypot, much more introverted and obviously insecure about his place. His idolaters at Stradey – the home where he was warm and snug and comfy and, as a result, glistening daring week after week – worried as much as he did whether he could take control in the genuine big time. A week after the match against England, there was staged the traditional farewell match for the tourists against the flamboyant scratch team, the Barbarians, at the Arms Park. Usually the thing is a fiesta, an exhibition, but this time – especially after a more than grumpy tour by the All Blacks – the Barbarians' finale was invested with the title 'Fifth Test Carried Over', meaning that the tourists were looking at it as a 'revenge' game for the singular beating the Lions had given them on their own patch less than eighteen months before. Accordingly, the Barbarians picked up the gauntlet and picked a dozen of those Lions – and also, uniquely for the olde-tyme ethos of the club, allowed Carwyn James to have a hand in the pre-match 'coaching'. Bennett was picked as pivot and playmaker. He was very, very nervous.

'Well, I knew I would be out of it, estranged. It wouldn't have been too bad to be on the wing, but so evidently replacing Barry preyed on my mind. I couldn't even find the ground when we were called for training at Penarth.'

Before the start, James quietly said his 'few words' in the dressing room, particularly singling out the 'self-estranged' Bennett.

The ballads. The hymns. The presentations. The expectations. Of a sudden, the rafter-packed throng is momentarily silent – and then, as Bennett kicks off, it is to a great wall of presumptive sound...

There is that routine first exchange of push and shove, with the ball almost ignored as the two sets of forwards lock horns and flex muscles and spirits... a set scrum, another general affray, then a maul – and the All Blacks have it; the mighty captain, Ian Kirkpatrick, has wrestled it free and is in open ground, blindside going right towards the river end. A decent pass, making space, to his right-wing, the ripping Samoan Bryan Williams, who carves up the touchline, past halfway, then steeples up a perfectly angled diagonal kick towards the Baa-Baas' posts, over the cover defence. It lands, exactly midfield, on the twenty-five-yard line, and daps once, twice, invitingly towards the posts as the New Zealanders greedily pursue it *en masse*. The Barbarians have to turn, pronto. One minute into the grudge match, and this could be seriously dangerous... Bennett is first to spot the danger, and first to the difficult bobbler, midway between his posts and the twenty-five, knowing this furious wave of adrenalin-charged All Blacks are bearing down on his back, to be sure, can only be yards away...

He gathers the ball, and, as he turns – rather, in the very act of turning – he drives his right foot into the ground fiercely, which causes him to pirouette and face the enemy, one of whom is already there. No, he isn't, he's already done for with that first magical hopscotch step... But here's another... again a mesmerizing right-foot sidestep and then, unbelievably, another... and another.

He is in the clear now, with room to bang the thing into touch and bow low at the wall of applause. But he doesn't.

What had Carwyn told him before he went out? So, still inside his twenty-five, he passes to his full-back, the onliest J.P.R.Williams, a yard or two on his left...

And thus Phil Bennett, nervous, shy and presuming himself to be overawed in such company, announced himself to the wider world. The try which resulted from that voluptuous and bespoke bit of tailoring by Bennett has been reprised and enthused over more, far more, times than any other single incident in all rugby history. It was scored by Gareth Edwards; it co-starred Williams, John Pullin, John Dawes, Tom David and Derek Quinnell; but it was undoubtedly – and the full cast all agree – Conceived, Produced and Directed by Philip Bennett, of Felinfoel, on the Llanelli—Carmarthen road.

It was nice, too, that one Cliff Morgan, of Trebanog and the BBC, was in the television commentary box to relate the facts. This is what he said: '...Kirkpatrick...to Bryan Williams, this is great stuff... Phil Bennett covering..., chased by Alistair Scown... brilliant... oh, that's brilliant... John Williams... Pullin... John Dawes, great dummy... David, Tom David, the halfway line... brilliant, by Quinnell... this is Gareth Edwards... a dramatic start... WHAT A SCORE!'

To this day, and typically, Bennett himself plays down his part in that explosively memorable twelve-second passage: 'At the time I was intent only on getting out of trouble. I sensed they were right on top of me. Perhaps the whole beautiful, amazing thing wouldn't have happened if I hadn't heard Alistair Scown's menacing footsteps bearing down on me. As it was, it was a bit of a hospital pass I gave to J.P.R., wasn't it?'

John Williams chips in: 'Well, certainly I nearly lost my head as Bryan Williams lunged at me. But what utter brilliance by Phil. I remain convinced that the whole thing was really Carwyn James's try. Unique to the Barbarians, who disapproved of coaching, they asked him to give us a talk before the game.'

'There was a lot of needle in the game; both us and the All Blacks were treating it as an unofficial fifth Test decider after we [the Lions] had beaten them, coached by Carwyn, eighteen months before. Now, before we went out, Carwyn soothed us, calming and relaxed, told us to enjoy it; and I'll never forget his last words, to insist to Phil, who was full of trepidation, hadn't played long for Wales and certainly not for the Lions, to go out and play just like he did for Llanelli

– every Saturday – "You're not in the shadows any more, Phil bach, go and show the world what Stradey knows".'

Up in the press box, as the applause battered on, sat Carwyn James. He was silent, staring. He took a long, deep, satisfied pull on his Senior Service. He inhaled and then, as he let the smoke waft out of his nose and mouth, a close observer could notice just a split second snake's-lick of a very private, very contented smile. In his weekly column in the following Friday's *Guardian*, he was to write of the moment, 'rare and unforgettable, when you can play at a level outside the conscious; when everything is instinct, but as clear as a bell because you have practised it so often and, especially, dreamed it – that unique moment when sport, lovely sport, not only achieves, but assumes, an art form.'.

from *The Great Number Tens* (1993)

EDDIE BUTLER

Prosser's Pontypool

Pontypool left the 1950s and slid away in the 1960s until they found themselves approaching the age of the Coach, the Cup and the general brilliance of the 1970s from the bottom of a grim pile-up. At the start of the golden decade they were adrift in that awful, lonely place known as Below Penarth. That is the moment when Ray Prosser was appointed coach. Now the age of legend could really begin. And here surely there was no room whatsoever for any ambiguity.

Pross was a single-minded monster, a rock in the second row who had been the one guaranteed supplier of possession for Benny [Jones] and the three-quarter jets in the 1950s. At some stage of his upbringing somebody had inserted railway sleepers where his shoulders should have been. He had played on twenty-two occasions for Wales between 1956 and 1961, a lock converted to prop for international duty. He was hard and crude, skilled and analytical. He was an enforcer and a technician, but only, it seemed, with regard to eight-fifteenths of the side. He professed always to have a fearful mistrust of three-quarters.

He was above all a character. And if much of his colour

came from his use of language – Anglo-Saxon at its most effluent, an invective that would draw crowds in their hundreds to the Park on training nights and which could cripple the feeble of spirit at fifty paces – much, too, came from his self-projection as the small-town simpleton. Pross could just about make it five miles up or down the valley, north to Blaenavon Forgeside where he would supervise Sunday morning gallops led by John Perkins high up on the tramways above Big Pit, or south to Cwmbran, but any further than these neighbouring towns in the Eastern Valley and he would fall victim to homesickness. In later years, after his career had progressed from driving a bulldozer to overseeing slag-reclamation at Panteg Steelworks, he would talk of his dislike for the weekly thirty-mile round-trip to Cardiff to pick up the wages.

'Yes, it must be worrying, Pross, having the responsibility for all that money, and you not particularly fond of driving.' 'Bollocks to the money,' Pross would say. 'It's just that Cardiff is such a long way away.'

He hated flying even more than driving, he claimed. They once managed to strap him into an aircraft seat for a tour to Washington D.C. in 1977, but he swore that he would never go into the air again.

And yet... and yet. In summer months his great frame could sometimes be found lying flat out, creating a bow in the warm corrugated-iron roof of his little hut with its stove- pipe chimney among the mountains of slag at the far end of the steelworks. He would be staring straight up into the sky. High above him would be the vapour trails of the flight path to and from the New World, and at their head distant silver specks of flying machines. Pross would know not just every passing plane by its shape – 747, DC10, Concorde, Airbus – but also its specifications and, above all, its safety record. What he feared became the object of serious study.

And as for being a small-town simpleton, it was to some extent true that when he had toured New Zealand with the Lions of 1959, he had pined for home. But it was also true that he spent a large period of the tour in hospital, and that while he was there he dedicated himself once again to serious study, this time of the rugby of the New Zealanders and, in particular, their forwards.

He analysed the New Zealand game from his hospital bed, went home, played on, retired and stepped back for further contemplation. Pontypool went into decline and all the while the coach-to-be stayed away and formulated his coaching philosophy. No doubt, just as he would do with his jet planes, he investigated specifications and performance. Only this time he was not so concerned about the issue of safety. The giant of post-war rugby in Pontypool crossed his bridge from playing days to coaching career.

It was the start of the 1970s and Welsh rugby was embarking on something gloriously adventurous on the international stage; brilliance and self-confidence were to make the age glitter. Pontypool, typically, were at the rock bottom of the club ladder. Below everyone. Brilliance was for others. Pross started to climb by another route, up a more extreme col. The country was starting to gasp at the exploits of Edwards and John and Gerald and J.P.R., Pross, however, needed forwards and he needed backs who would be subservient to his forwards.

From Newport he garnered such backs as centre Ivor Taylor who would become his right-hand man later on the coaching front. But most important of all he welcomed home Terry Cobner after the latter concluded his teachers' training course at Madeley College near Stoke-on-Trent. Cobner of Blaenavon became the on-field inspiration from wing-forward and captain of the new Pontypool.

It seemed that Pross had not had to move outside his self-proclaimed five-mile exclusion zone, although perhaps he extended it to ten miles for that rarer commodity, a back in the county who fitted his bill. Once again, however, it is worth pointing out that while Pontypool truly developed a game that was exclusively theirs – a sort of evolutionary blip, as if they were up some deep-sided valley off-shoot where the sun never shone and that time had forgotten – the reality is that Pontypool never suffered from such acute introspection or even geographic isolation.

Travel north from Pontypool towards Abergavenny and to the left rise Mynydd Garnclochty and the Blorenge Mountain, high ridges over which lies Blaenavon, a town of coal and iron. But from right on top of the mountain, at the Keeper's Pond, a reservoir whose waters used to be piped down to the town and the water-balance tower at its forges, the view reveals that this is the first ridge of the industrial valleys of Wales. To the right of the Pontypool-Abergavenny road lies the rolling pasture-land of the Vale of Usk. Pontypool is not confined by twin steep sides. It has always enjoyed flat access to Monmouthshire and the Forest of Dean. There are even in the Eastern Valley accent certain similarities to the drawl of the Forest in terms of quirky grammar, like the use of 'be' for 'is'. The Pontypool voice is obviously Welsh but it is closer to the sounds of Coleford than to the nasal strains of Newport to the south.

It is more than accent. Strong rugby connections exist between the easternmost club in Wales and the clubs of the West Country of England. This story will reveal how relations between the Pooler and many, many clubs grew strained to breaking point, but Gloucester were always strong allies. There were wonderful nights at Kingsholm, of baying crowds and unfettered mischief, of huge confrontation and regular reductions to fourteen players per side. More recently, Bath have been stout supporters of Pontypool's latest drive, in 1998, to climb out of crisis. And closest of all were Berry Hill, from within the boundaries of the royal forest itself, who were like blood brothers, even on the day of the game against the Pontypool second XV, the Athletic, when play was stopped for a search to be conducted in the mud for half an ear. It was a day of brown and crimson hues in the Park.

For the moment, though, at the outset of the Prosser years, isolation referred only to Pontypool's position in the pecking order of Welsh clubs. They were adrift at the bottom. Cobner soon changed all that. Pontypool climbed to eighth in the unofficial championship. The next season they were champions.

There was local talent on tap. Graham Price was playing in the front row as a teenager, a slender, curly-blonde prop on orange squash, who would go home after each game shaking with exhaustion. Ron Floyd, Bill Evans – an outsider from as far away as Abergavenny – and soon John Perkins, another to make the short trip down from Blaenavon, filled the second row.

The message from Pross to his charges was straightforward: utter devotion to the collective cause. In the summer he flogged them up and down the Grotto, a gruelling run from the pitch up to the then ruined Folly Tower – a hilltop landmark rebuilt in recent years, having been destroyed by the army in 1940 to prevent enemy bombers using it as a beacon on their way to the munitions works at Glascoed – and in the winter the forwards themselves flogged other packs at the scrummage.

The anonymous efficiency of the Pontypool pack had its advantages and disadvantages. Ron Floyd was picked to play for Wales B against France B away, a just reward for the big lock's largely unseen contributions at club level. On the eve of the match, as the players of both sides stood awkwardly at some mayoral get-together in the local town-hall, one of the Welsh selectors approached the tall, swarthy man of Gwent and with great deliberation asked him, '*Bonsoir*, do you speak English?'

Pontypool were operating at full power. The pack was awesome at the scrummage, fearsome at the line-out, destructive at the ruck. Full-back Robin Williams kicked goals from anywhere inside seventy yards from the opposition posts, equally adept and long-distanced with either left or right foot. Terry Cobner was immense on the charge, hugely strong and with a centre of gravity as low as his boot-laces. But perhaps the power would never have truly been galvanized without the arrival of two players in those rebuilding years of the early 1970s. Two-thirds of the Pontypool front row. They came from the town of Newport via the rugby club of Cross Keys. Yes, Pontypool was transformed for ever when Bobby Windsor and Tony 'Charlie' Faulkner turned up.

Graham Price in those early days was, as suggested, pushing uphill in the grown-up game. He was a local pup, a product of West Mon. School in the town, destined to become one of the Rolls-Royce players of his generation. He was to be a player way ahead of his time, a prop as fast as a back-row with handling skills to match, a tight-head who would win a record number of caps for his position – forty-one between his debut in 1975 at the age of twenty-two and 1983 – and who would play in twelve Lions tests, another record for a prop, on three tours between 1977 and 1983. But three years before his debut for Wales he needed help in the Pontypool front row. It came in the form of a double-act: 'The Duke' at hooker and 'Charlie' on the loose head. Pricey was the quiet one; the other two spiced things up.

They were not that big, although Bobby, when he came home from the Lions tour of 1974, was eighteen stone of world-class athletic venom. Charlie had a strange bottom half to his body, or maybe it just looked slightly spindly compared to his torso from the middle of his back upwards. He was fantastically strong around the shoulders and neck, and if Bobby had an utterly ruthless edge, Charlie had the martial arts of karate. To be fair, he never seemed to use them on the field to hurt people; he preferred to employ more straightforward arts when it came to dishing out pain. Charlie became well-known for his reply to the press when asked about the skills of scrummaging: 'Up, down, inside out – anywhere but backwards.' But he also had another phrase, which he would shout out in the club if anyone asked him about his days in the Territorial Army. He would remember nocturnal patrols in Gibraltar: '*Alto. Arriba las manos o disparo*'. (Stop. Put your hands up or I'll shoot).

They were certainly not angelic. When I first joined the club in 1976 there was a story going round that the pair of them had been taken in for questioning by the police over some minor misunderstanding. Nothing serious, but it was essential that they synchronized their stories. After the briefest time to prepare, they were led into different rooms and asked to give their accounts separately. Remarkably, every detail of two highly convoluted tales matched perfectly. Except for the moment when a cat had apparently run in front of their car. Bobby said it was black, Charlie said it was white. They were hauled back in for round 2. The colour of the cat was a serious stumbling point. Was it black or was it white? 'Ah, that,' said Charlie. 'Well, you have to remember, it was a very frosty night.'

On the field they could be lethal, although it must be said that they respected the conventions of the battlefield. I once played in a second team game alongside Bobby after we were well past our retirement date, a long time even after the day on tour in Canada in 1985 when he became a grandfather and a father on the same day. Anyway, the Athletic were playing against Tredegar and Bobby simply could not resist giving their scrum-half a little belt. The scrum-half, suitably annoyed, waited and waited until the coast was clear and gave Bob his best shot in return. A neat punch, too. At that moment the referee blew his whistle for the end of the game, and Bob set off after the scrum-half, who not surprisingly had headed for the safety of the tunnel. Suddenly the Pontypool hooker with a trickle of blood coming from his nose was alongside him. The scrum- half turned to run again, but Bob reached out and grabbed him. 'Game's over, Ian,' he said. The scrum-half looked even more worried. 'No, I mean that's it. Whistle's gone, time for a pint, no hard feelings.'

Those hard feelings were reserved for the field of play. There was a time in the mid-1970s when the scrummage was nigh-on uncontrollable, so fast would the front five propel it forward. Oh, in big Cup games the opposition would raise their game and hold firm and Pontypool would be denied yet again a taste of the high life, but in the course of a season's bread-and-butter fixtures, the pack would generate a special quiver, just prior to the put-in by the other team's scrum-half, which meant that the timing of the drive was just right and that somebody had better watch out because rib cartilage was liable to pop. It was the elevation of a humdrum restart activity to some sort of Stalinist collectivist ideal whose goal is the pure joy of destruction...

from *Heart and Soul* (1998)

RUPERT MOON WITH DAVID ROACH

Moonstruck

I can see the tunnel stretching in front of me and I can hear the noise from the crowd, booming like a tidal wave, sucking me forward onto the pitch. I feel sick. I don't want to go out there but I have to. I'm fighting every instinct in my body, desperate to stay safe in the shadows. Can I leave now? Can I go home? Please, let me go? No. No, this is where I will define myself. A calmness takes over and smothers my anxiety. I want this. I want what's out there waiting for me. My mind jolts, I can't catch my breath, I'm running... someone is shouting, I can hear the studs clattering up the tunnel, scraping, slipping... and suddenly, I'm in daylight and the noise of the howling thousands batters me into submission. I am in the moment. I have over fifty thousand reasons to be here. I have a purpose. I have a job to do.

The anthems are over and done with before I know it. I can't hear a thing. Did I sing? I'm sure I sang; I'd put too much effort into understanding the words not to sing, but I can't remember singing. We huddle, I'm shouting, I'm not making any sense but I'm saying all the right things. I'm looking at Emyr Lewis and Ricky Evans, John Davies and Scott

Quinnell. What am I saying? They are listening to me with their eyes. I can't hear what I'm saying. Where's Andy Nichol? He's good... sneaky, quick, smart thinking. What's he doing? What's he saying to his pack? No, don't look at them. Don't let them see you, stay hidden, stay secret. Be invisible. Emerge from the forwards like an extra flanker and be big, be bigger and taller, faster and braver than any other player in this arena. My mouth isn't saying what I'm thinking. 'Okay, this is it, boys. I love you, we're off. Let's do them.'

It's wet, the ball is wet. My hands are wet. The ball is too wet. There is water in my eyes. My studs are slipping. There's water in my socks already and we've just started. Where's the ball? Where is it? 'Pegs, where's the ball?' Here's the ball, it's coming now... here it is! Here's the ball. Right, it's mine. Look, pass, where's Jinks? No... he doesn't want it. Where's Nichol? Get it out, just get it out! Go, Ieuan, now. Ball, boot, and kick... yes, solid shot, is that more rain? Stay in play ball, stay in... go, Ieuan, go! Come on, boys, after it... in there...' Ouch. Punches, get in there, take the punch, it doesn't hurt, you can't hurt me, no one can, my body is on the line, show them you can't hurt me. Hit me again, go on, can't hurt me, hit me! Look at Garin! He's going mad, punching, punching, punching... punching. Whistle. French ref. Shouting... '*Non!*' '*Non!*' I'm in, scragged, someone's flung me on my butt. On the grass... it's so wet! Who did that? Who did that? Logan? 'Logan, you little... was that you, Logan?' He's walking away, smiling. Got me. Get up quick, I look stupid. 'Ref, ref, no, ref... Garin... it's cool, Garin's cool.' Walk away, leave. Don't look, don't think. Breathe, Rupert. Breathe. Breathe.

from *Full Moon* (2003)

RICHARD DAVIES

Gone from under your nose

It is late summer. This year I'm living in a new town. A compact little town near the mouth of a river. It is not home. The hills are too small and we are too close to the sea. But I'm here with my family, a big house on the same street as the school and the swimming pool.

The rugby pitch is just up on the Aberystwyth road. It sits square in the town secured by space, a clubhouse and a stand. I've looked at it as I drive to the beach. Most days it is empty. Sometimes there's a couple of boys kicking a football around. There doesn't seem to be any sign of the team.

I read the first match reports in the paper. The team is off to a winning start. On the third Saturday of September I watch the second team play Tenby. It is a close game on a hard ground. At half-time Cardigan make too many changes. Tenby stick to their team. They haven't brought any substitutes. Ten minutes into the second half Tenby have scored three tries as Cardigan fail to reorganise themselves with the new faces. The game is over. I watch the last thirty minutes. No one knows me here. I have not brought my kit. I've packed it in. The last twenty years of weekly training and Saturday matches just stopped on a whim of age.

The smells come back to me. A crowded dressing room, deep heat, bandages. The rituals of preparation. Men joined in a community of ritual. Everyone knows their role, position, job. There is a challenge to be met.

I remember a game late in the season when the referee made a statement to the changing room that he knew it was going to be a tough game but 'Please nothing stupid, boys, we've all got work in the morning.'

It is a game and more than a game. I was part of a club for twenty years. My father's name was on the captains' board in the 60s, my uncle's for a few seasons in the early 70s. My father had built the club – he was a builder and he put it up with a few mates on the weekends. To be part of the club was to be part of a society with its own rules. Traditions, memories, stories.

I had been taken to watch games as a six-year-old. My father was the coach by then. I didn't pay much attention but there was usually a wood next to the away ground where I could play and there was always faggots and peas and coke and crisps after the game.

I grew up with the game around. Uncles and cousins all played. It was in the paper, on the news. On international days we drew the heavy curtains of the living room and watched the TV. Then school. There was always a school team. I didn't enjoy it much. I was scared and unfit. The game hurt. There were boys with growth hormone problems who were 6ft tall when the rest of us were 5ft 3ins. But it was part of me and I couldn't miss the challenge. All the teachers knew my father. I was expected to play.

In a tough valley we played the other schools. I remember losing 72-0 to Llangatwg when tries were worth four points and they didn't bother kicking conversions. The sheer terror of trying to catch a ball with the big, hairy, surely overage forwards massing on the far side, only ten short yards away. At least at school the opposition were likely to be the same age. In club rugby the under 13 front row for Seven Sisters were all shaving.

We eventually caught up with Llangatwg as we produced a hormone success of our own in the shape of Lyndon Jones. A fierce bull of a fifteen-year-old boy, Lyndon was known to turn up for a Saturday morning game after a heavy night of drinking on the town. He was often covered in love bites and once, before a Sevens tournament in Hereford, produced a used condom out of the pocket of his duffel coat. At fifteen I had never seen a condom or kissed a girl. There seemed more chance of a trip to the moon.

The fear of seeing Lyndon Jones, all six foot fourteen stone of him running towards me on a training field finally receded a few months later when he fell over me in my attempt to get out of his way. The games teacher, Dai Will, shouted 'Good tackle, Richard' and I realised if you put enough bulk in front of something it will usually stop them. I tried this ten years later, trying to stop Dale Mackintosh, a monstrous but friendly New Zealander playing for Pontypridd. The club still owes me the dental bills. You've got to tackle forward not backwards.

School moved to youth rugby – a whole new set of rules. Older boys – still boys – and better singing, more drinking. Wales has a culture of youth that is centred on drinking. How much you can drink before falling over is seen as an attainment. This pervades all rugby in Wales and youth rugby was soaked in it.

At this point in life I didn't enjoy alcohol. I made a point of avoiding it. I was the only rugby player in the team who didn't drink. This lasted a year. I'm not sure about the standard of the rugby but my drinking improved.

And then rugby is a process of growing up and leaving. I had a few choices given by education. To leave Wales and study in London. I played for London Welsh in an under 21 team of New Zealanders, Englishmen, Australians, South Africans and a vague north Walian. It was great rugby. I made some good friends in six months with boys I have never seen again.

Somehow I returned home after university. I got a job on a building site with my father. I was back playing with the same boys who had been in the school and then youth team. We were older. Just a few years. Most of us played for the second team. There were men in the first team. Men thirty years old with muscles, real muscles and a toughness that comes with ten years of hard labour or ten years of just playing rugby on a Saturday afternoon. The men had wives and children. Some already bore some of the scars. You can get hurt playing against men.

I can go on with this but it is my story. One of thousands. I wrote a book about it. Losing, winning. My concerns at the time; work, sex and rugby.

It is the moments that stay with you. The days in the rain. A high ball caught running backwards towards the post against New Dock Stars. Finally winning away against Banwen, shouting to myself as I drove out of the village on a Saturday night after the game, elation. A dummy which sent me in under the posts against Tonna Seconds. Running out under lights for Pontypridd, the big time, the first xv. One game. Phil Vaughan congratulating me in the Bryncoch clubhouse after winning a game against Seven Sisters. Phil Vaughan was and is a hero of mine. Winning and losing. There are deep pleasures in victory, despair in losing, but you have to know both.

The final few years of playing, a synthesis of ideas. New directions, clearing the mind on a Saturday afternoon. Anything to play. The same joke every week in the showers. The men before us on the touchlines, the boys grown into men. Something in being part of the tribe. Sunday mornings always stiff with bruises, feeling alive. To play is it all.

Then it is gone from under your nose.

from *As I was a boy fishing* (2003)

JOHN STUART WILLIAMS

River Walk, Cardiff

Walking by the river, the morning cold
thick between old trees
dimly spread in parkland ease,
he stops to watch a mess of small
boys, a muddy ruck of all-sorts,
playing at playing rugby, hurts
and triumphs muffled in the turf.

The ball,
kicked true for once, hangs
in the lifting wind, gull without wings,
then drops dead in his unused hands.
The feel of it, the dubbined skin, sends old
signals through his fingers, cold
and clumsy, releases things long forgot,
the smell of wintergreen, the hot roar
of crowds, running in to score,
a snatch of rude song: a scene
that mocks the years in between, fall
of leaf, the cruel quickness of it all.

A clatter of startled rooks breaks
him free: he grins, wryly kicks
the ball back, resumes his steady walk.

from *Dic Penderyn and other poems* (1983)

LEWIS DAVIES

Training night

A dim security light faltered in the weak drizzle which darkened the tarmac of the club car park. Lewis waited patiently, reluctant to leave the warmth of his car. He counted three other vehicles. He knew the drivers and acknowledged Mike in the car next to him. He speculated, eight players here now, perhaps another six who would turn up. Fuck, what was he doing here? Another set of headlights illuminated the drizzle before a fat Ford Granada lumbered up outside the club building. The driver's door opened and the occupant disembarked with an air of importance that should have precluded his entry to anywhere as unglamorous as a rugby club on a Thursday night.

'Well at least that bastard's here,' commented Lewis to himself in the absence of anyone else in the car.

'Had to really, I suppose. He's got the bloody keys.'

Although it had been known to wait an hour for somebody to open the changing rooms.

The figure from the Granada walked disdainfully to the side entrance of the club building which abutted onto an open field, its boundaries lost from view in the drizzled darkness.

The changing room light elicited a similar response from the cars, flashing on then off again as the occupants made a dash for the club. Lewis was last to enter. The white-washed walls forced his eyes to readjust to the brightness just too quickly as a series of greetings and abuse greeted him.

'Awright, Lew?'

'Hi'ah Mike.'

'Hi'ah, Lew.'

'Lew.'

'Awright, pal.'

'What a night for training, ay.'

Lewis tried to instill some enthusiasm into his voice that he didn't feel. There was no reply – it was a mutual feeling. He settled down into the corner of the changing room, unwilling to begin undressing and start the training ordeal. He stared in isolation at a piece of dried mud on the bare concrete floor. The changing room hadn't been cleaned since Saturday and the desiccated mud, discarded from a boot in the aftermath of a match now lay brittle on the floor. A number of petrified circular shapes betrayed its provenance. Lewis's eyes remained fixed upon it, already a relic from a long-forgotten never-recalled match. He wondered how much mud had been swept away from the changing room every week for thirty years. Thirty years of endeavour in the search of enjoyment. How many more countless Saturday afternoons? He spat viciously at the dried mud, his saliva forming globules which rolled and stuck in the dust. He rubbed the saliva and dried earth into the concrete floor with his trainer and watched as the brittle mud became malleable again.

'Ay Lew, you getting changed or what?'

The sharp question roused him from his reverie. He looked up resignedly.

'Aye, I suppose I better had,' he replied without any conviction. He was still reluctant to leave the warmth of his clothes and the soft heat of his thoughts.

Most of the other lads were changing, but there was no urgency in their actions. No one really wanted to train, not tonight. It was cold, wet and miserable; the enthusiasm was infectious. They were all ill with it. Reluctance pervaded every movement and spoken word. The season had become a burden, it had not been a good one. Relegation beckoned unless they won on Saturday but no one cared anymore. The majority didn't even train now. The boys who persevered loved the game or at least loved their wives less. Training was a good excuse for an evening's escape. For the unmarried ones it was a useful time filler before they ventured into town, always good for a laugh on a Thursday night.

The scrape of aluminium on the cold, earth-covered floor mingled with the occasional comment and meaningless banter that vied uneasily with the silence, as the varied occupants of the changing room changed into their one unifying element: rugby players.

'Anyone coming out?' Mike enquired to no one in particular. There was no reply.

'C'mon, boys, let's get out there.'

Lewis would have gone but he hadn't finished lacing his boots.

'Give it five, mun, Mike. It's bloody freezing out there,' requested a squat man through the tangle of an improbable beard.

Lewis looked up at Rod and smiled in admiration. Rod was a regular; he turned up every week. In fact he had turned up every week for the last fifteen years. He was well into his thirties and still enjoyed the game. But it was an admiration tinged with horror at the inevitability of it all. Would he really be doing this for that long, there had to be some progression. Well, there was always the committee.

Lewis tied up his thoughts with his bootlaces.

'C'mon, then, let's get it over with.'

There was a shuffle towards the door. Mike had already gone out and was now kicking the ball high up into the air and catching it again. The remainder of the occupants of the changing room gave in to the inevitable and trudged out onto the field.

Lewis felt the drizzle absorb him in its soft wetness as it clung to his jersey and the hairs on his legs. The weak training lights struggled to illuminate the pitch, one corner was almost dark where one of the bulbs had failed while the remainder of the pitch was bathed in a half light that endeavoured to keep the darkness at its edges. Around the lights the drizzle appeared to form concentric circles as the specks drifted to the ground. Towards the end of the season the pitch, never lavishly turfed, suffered through over-use and degenerated into a treacherous quagmire. The remaining isolated patches of grass caught the drizzle which then shimmered in the reflected lustre of the floodlights.

A number of players teed balls up on the mud before attempting to kick them between the uprights. The efforts were of widely varying quality, the big forwards illustrated clearly why they were never given the honour on a Saturday afternoon with a variety of grasscutters, improbable hooks and wide slices. While Saturday's regular kicker proceeded to demonstrate that without the pressure of a game and a crowd he could sail the conversions effortlessly through the uprights. But come Saturday when the real thing presented itself he would once again be reduced to an erratic hit and hope merchant.

Lewis wasn't interested in the kicking. He was realistic about his chances of having a go on Saturday and as a result he stood around, waiting for something more interesting to happen. He exchanged a few platitudes with some of the players who were waiting for a spare ball to kick at the posts but no one was interested in conversation.

'Game of touch, boys?' proposed Mike hopefully. There was little response. One or two heads turned but most of the fourteen or so players continued with aimless conversion practice.

Mike tried again. 'Let's get a game going, boys.' His suggestion again met with a muted response. But a few bodies gradually began to drift towards the centre of the pitch. Mike sensed his chance; announced with some authority. 'Stripes against plains, then.'

Everyone instinctively looked at their jerseys to see what side they were on. 'Stripes up that end.'

Two sides gradually separated to their respective halves of the pitch except Daz, the regular kicker, who was still trying to redeem himself for Saturday's dreadful miss in front of the post by kicking conversions from increasingly unlikely angles. Nobody was watching him, however, as Alfie Edwards was hovering nervously around the halfway line undecided over which side to join.

'What's up, Alfie?' questioned Mike, who was busily giving his side the game plan.

'Well, I'm not sure what side I'm on.'

There was a general round of laughter at Alfie's pronouncement. Alfie wasn't sharp and it showed.

'Well what jersey have you got on?' asked Mike in disbelief.

'Well it's sort of banded,' replied Alfie defensively to more general laughter.

'Up here, mun, Alfie,' shouted one of the stripes. Alfie, relieved to receive an instruction, began to jog up towards the stripes when one of the plains shouted.

'Don't listen to them, Alf, you're on our side, down 'ere, mun.'

Alfie stopped, engulfed in agonies of indecision.

'No, up 'ere mun Alf, stripes you've got on.'

'Down 'ere Alf.'

'C'mon Alfie, you're on our side.'

'Don't desert us, Alf.'

There was a general humour in the banter that Alfie missed completely. Lewis smiled in sympathy with Alfie but was unable to prevent himself from enjoying his predicament.

Mike settled the issue. 'You're on our side, Alfie: we're one short.'

The comments died away as Alfie joined the plains. Mike shouted for the ball which Daz reluctantly kicked to him. The game was about to start when someone objected to the arbitrary make-up of the sides. Lewis would have given up at this point but Mike persevered through another two minutes of argument during which Dai Philips changed sides twice before the game finally started.

Touch rugby was a favourite on a Thursday night. It involved little effort and almost no physical contact. It was hardly useful training for the match on Saturday but then nobody pretended it was.

The game had only been going five minutes when Lewis noticed a rotund figure in an ill-fitting tracksuit emerge from the changing rooms. It was Dai Fats; the name encapsulated his appearance. It wasn't that he was overweight; he was weight. His tracksuit failed miserably to cover his belly which protruded in the form of a large spherical object and had all the characteristics of a stick-on appendage. Fats was someone who put a lot of time and effort into his physique. He could usually be found propping up the bar on a time-share basis, but was known to avoid the training pitch with a rare commitment despite his nominal role as club coach. Fats was a dying breed: a dinosaur of a coach soon to be replaced by fitness coordinators and physios who ran leisure centres in their spare time. Most of the other teams already had a reputable coach: someone with first-class experience or even a minor ex-international. Fats's qualifications were based on a few unsuccessful youth team appearances before he graduated to the beery slob and barstool expert which he was now. In addition to a total lack of appreciation for the game he viewed most matches through an alcohol haze which was duly reflected in his training techniques and subsequent team selections. But although Fats stuck to his title with a rare resolution, in reality he knew he was on the way out and this season's imminent relegation would seal it. He had probably already settled for a selectorial role on the committee.

As he waddled closer several of the players realised with horror who he was and the game of touch gradually slowed to a standstill. He hadn't been out for a few weeks, citing a strained back muscle and he had never been known to come out on a Thursday. But he was no mirage. Down to his black and white bobble cap protecting his diminishing head of hair he was real and striding purposefully towards them, obviously intent on a last ditch attempt to avert relegation and maintain his personal source of international tickets.

Dai Fats needlessly announced his arrival on the field with a sharp blast on a whistle. The players shuffled around uneasily.

'Right then, four laps to warm up,' he bellowed across the pitch.

Mike jogged off instantly and the others grudgingly followed him while complaining bitterly to each other over the presence of Fats. There were not enough players to go through any meaningful practice moves while a fitness session with the game two days away would be useless. Lewis kept his thoughts to himself. He was aware of the futility of Fats's appearance but was still encouraged by his presence.

They knocked off the four laps easily with only two stragglers falling behind a comfortable pace. Fats stood motionless on the halfway line, only his head following the players progress as they ran around the perimeter of the pitch. As they jogged in, Fats imperiously announced a series of indeterminate sprints. Lewis could feel the reluctance stifle his stride as he accelerated the thirty yards of sprinting distance. An aversion to the training hung malignantly between the players. They were the ones out on a Thursday night and here they were getting bollocked for it.

Fats stood impassively on the halfway line periodically blasting his whistle between hoarse shouts of disparagement at the players' efforts.

'You're all too bloody slow,' he announced. 'No wonder you're bottom of the league.'

'I'd like to see that bastard come 'ere and try a sprint, just one,' cursed Daz.

'He's too fat to fucking run,' asserted Rod.

'Only time he runs is when it's his fucking round; you won't catch the bastard then.'

There was a round of laughter at the much abused joke.

'Right then, sixty yards now,' announced Fats with rancour coursing through his voice as he moved a further thirty yards away. The sprinting continued. Lewis was careful. He was fit: fit enough to cope with anything Fats could dream up and so were most of the boys. There was no point in killing themselves before the game on Saturday.

'Take it easy, boys; just stride it out. Don't worry about Fats; he'll soon head for the bar.'

Forty minutes later they were still running. The comments of muted disapproval had become threats of open mutiny. If they were to be believed a horrible death awaited Fats when he finally finished the training session. Fats had now resumed his position on the halfway line, his inert form occasionally bursting into a sequence of frenzied arm waving and side stretching. This he considered more than sufficient to maintain his fitness level. On this point, for one of the rare occasions in his life, he was right.

'Come on in then, boys. I want to say a few words about Saturday's game.'

The players reluctantly converged on Fats. A crowd shuffled around him, breathing heavily from their exertions. Viewed from a distance, the group appeared to be engulfed in a cloud of steam as their warm breath condensed in the sharp night air. Fats waited for a lull in the mutterings of discontent which lurked just below the surface of resentful attention. But as no lull appeared, he started his speech regardless.

'Right then, boys. You don't need me to tell you how fucking important this fucking game is for us on fucking Saturday.' Fats expected no reply and there wasn't any, save for a few embarrassed sideways glances. His use of adjectives was not extensive but he stuck with the ones he knew best and trusted. Fats continued. 'I've just got one fucking thing to say: if that fucking Dunvant outfit come up here Saturday thinking they can fucking win they've got another fucking think coming. Right?'

There was no reply to Fats in full flow. 'We're going to show

84

them what fucking rugby in this valley is all about. We'll show them who can fucking play rugby. So get tuned in now and no fucking drinking on Friday night.'

With this final outline of Saturday's match plan Fats turned and headed for the bar. During the speech Lewis had difficulty containing his laughter which he had only drowned with a rising reservoir of contempt for the fallacy of the man.

'Right then, lads. We all know what we've got to do on Saturday: fuck them and there's no problem,' summarised Daz.

The group barely laughed as they gratefully made for the haven of the changing rooms. Only Mike remained to practice his kicking for Saturday.

The showers were a misnomer, involving only a tepid trickle of reluctant water. They were fitted in a hurry thirty years ago and might have been reasonable for a year or two but now only coughed and spluttered through rusting heads. It was necessary to get in early to catch the limited amount of water heated by the languid boiler, but even this was welcome after the long training session. Lewis relaxed under the weak but regular head he had claimed. The water splashed off his head and onto his back. The sensation was the most welcome of the evening. In the half-light he tried to remove as much mud as he could see.

'Coming down town tonight, Lew?' enquired Daz.

Lewis rinsed the shampoo from his eyes before replying. 'Where you thinking of going?'

'The Arch probably.'

'Aye, might as well, I suppose. Mike coming down?'

'No, I don't think so. He's saving his money for Saturday.'

'What for? It's his stag night, we'll be buying the drinks.'

'C'mon, Lew, you know his girlfriend. She won't let him out on a Thursday night with all those loose women around.'

'How does she know they're all loose?'

'That's where she met him, didn't she?' concluded Daz.

Lewis didn't reply, only smiled. 'I suppose he'll give us a lift into town though.'

'Aye, he should do. Ask him when he comes in.'

Lewis was half-dressed before Mike appeared in the changing rooms from his kicking practice. The showers were now cold.

'Ay, Mike, give us a lift into town will you?'

'Yeh sure, Lew. Going to leave your car here, are you?'

'Aye, I'll pick it up in the morning. We'll be in the bar, right.'

from *Work, Sex and Rugby* (1993)

ALUN RICHARDS

The flat on the Via I Monti

'Come to Italy?'

I was not very keen.

'Why not?'

'Don't fancy it.'

'Come on! I'll have a flat. You can work in the mornings. Rovigo's in the North.'

'What's it like?'

'Just like Llanelli!'

'That rules it out then. If it was like Pontypridd, I might be tempted.' Where Welshmen are concerned, a blade of grass can form the frontier making foreign territory.

'Come on! You'll like it when you get there. They're very friendly people.'

'I'll see,' I said. 'Drop me a line when you arrive.'

'That'll be the day,' a mutual friend said.

Carwyn James was notorious for his unanswered letters. At this time in 1977, although I had met him previously and known of him for most of my adult life, I did not really know him. He was a West Walian and I am an East Walian, and, as

I was fond of telling him, we were as different as chalk and cheese. We had some things in common apart from a lifelong interest in rugby football. We had both been teachers, had both given up teaching – he, quite recently for journalism and broadcasting, whereas I had long since become a professional writer and, if I was known for anything in Wales, it was for my critical views of the Welsh Establishment. He, on the other hand, apart from his differences with the Welsh Rugby Union, was one of the most confident Welshmen of his generation and moved easily in those Welsh-speaking areas of Establishment Wales which, in my view, stubbornly refuse to admit that there is no greater dividing line than that formed by a language. It is a difficult thing to explain to an outsider, how a man can feel a stranger in his own country, and the indifference of many Welshmen to their nation springs from the feeling, often justified, of being excluded, especially from those organisations in broadcasting and education where executive positions and a good many others are reserved for those with bilingual qualifications. It is an old complaint, and a lost battle as far as many Welshmen are concerned, but Carwyn (who would not accept this view) was not only the epitome of Welsh-speaking Wales, a Welsh scholar, a chapel deacon and Plaid Cymru candidate, but an ex-Welsh-international fly-half, the triumphant coach of the 1971 British Lions in New Zealand and a regular broadcaster who brought wit and intelligence to bear on whatever subject he spoke about. He was a man always in demand, who crossed dividing lines with ease, and because of rugby football, one of the best-known men in Wales.

'Rovigo's near Venice and Padua. It won't just be rugby. There's the opera.'

'Duck-shooting as well, I expect?'

'Why not?

When Carwyn wanted something, he persisted. I did not realise it at the time, but I see now that he was then a man almost at the end of his tether. In the first place, it was a shock to see how physically unfit he was – and his general health never really improved. In the second, he felt a compulsion to get away from Wales, to breathe a different air, and what was to me a jaunt, was to him a need. He was going to be away for a year at least and wanted company.

Always a convivial presence, he is somehow permanently implanted in the memory, a glass in hand, wreathed in cigarette smoke, his figure well-rounded, suit a little crumpled, sometimes lacking a belt, perhaps a remote Queensland rugby club tie and shirt unbuttoned. It was as if he felt it was somehow very English to be absolutely impeccable. Not that appearances ever worried him, or those who most cared for him. It was his smile which was the most important thing. When he smiled, it was with his whole face, often nodding intently as if the smile was not enough, and he had the most infectious chuckle.

'If I send you a wire, will you come?'

'I'll think about it,' I said. He was what is known as a confirmed bachelor and I'd already had first-hand experience of the domestic duties imposed on his guests, for he was a man who regarded a tin opener as a complicated and highly technical instrument, the use of which required at least a degree in mechanical engineering. Once, at one of his many lodgings, he had been charged with the care of a cat bearing the unlikely name of Angharad Trenchard-Jones and, failing to open a tin of cat food, had substituted the Sunday joint. I hesitated also because I had a wife, children, and a novel to write.

But he rubbed his hands gleefully.

'Right! That's settled,' he said, as if a decision had been made. The same invitation had been extended to a number of people for he selected friends in much the same way a bibliophile might choose books for his library – in all, a great variety of people. He needed them all. But only a few came. When I got to know him well, one of the first things to surprise me was his vulnerability. In so many ways, he was a man who could not say no to people, and there were days when everybody seemed to impose upon him and his time.

At that time nobody could understand why he wanted to coach in Italy in the first place. As BBC Wales's rugby correspondent, his weekly match analyses on television were avidly awaited. He wrote occasional elegant essays for the *Guardian* on rugby football and had a summer brief to cover cricket. As a journalist and broadcaster he was constantly in demand, contributing to programmes of all kinds, and the summer before, he had covered the Commonwealth Games in Canada for BBC Wales. He was also constantly being asked to speak at functions and wherever he stayed, the telephone never seemed to stop ringing. And yet he was bored.

Wherever he went, especially in rugby clubs and particularly in Llanelli, he was the subject of adulation. He could not walk down the street without being stopped by a host of people anxious to hear his views, often forcibly expressing their own on this rugby topic or that. At parties, he was the centrepiece, his ear the most easily purloined, for he was the most remarkable and patient listener ever. In short, he was the man everybody wanted to speak to and, although he was several times accused of arrogance in his dealings with the Welsh Rugby Union, he was really a lifelong victim of his own nature. For there was in him a sensitivity that made him the prey of other people, a gentleness of nature that did not want to offend, the capacity for which he secretly admired in other people.

A month later, contrary to expectation, both the letter and the telegram arrived. I soon found myself stepping off the plane in Venice to see his enigmatic figure smiling broadly down from the privileged visitors' gallery where he stood in the same suit and yet another rugby club tie, this time in the presence of two huge South African forwards, Dirk Naude and Dries Cotzer, guest players for his new club, Sanson Rovigo.

The customs formalities were soon over. 'You didn't expect the telegram, did you?'

'No,' I said.

'That's East Wales, you see? Suspicious, always.'

'Not without justification.'

'Never mind, now we can leave all that behind us.' But we never did.

I often reminded him of Joyce's phrase which I transposed – Wales is an old sow that eats her own farrow – but he always laughed. Of all the people he knew, he said, we were both the most easily available for the dish. Neither of us had ever stayed away for long. Neither of us could ever pass as coming from anywhere else, like some of our more famous compatriots whom we jocularly regarded as light-skinned negroes passing as white. In private such inflammatory phrases delighted him and we had a mutual habit of collecting sentences most likely to give offence. His favourite was spoken to me, a rebellious figure glaring over the wardroom silver in Portsmouth years before.

'There's something in what you say, Richards, and no doubt you have your contribution to make, however small!'

Such sentences delighted him, largely, I suspect, because they were the antithesis of himself.

In Venice, we took a launch to see the sights, but sitting in a café opposite the Basilica of San Marco he soon asked if I had brought the *Western Mail* as ordered and immediately turned to the Welsh rugby club results. He took his own square mile of Wales with him wherever he went and remained intensely rooted, Wales-centred and Wales-dominated. Yet, as I came to think, that inevitable preoccupation wore him out, whereas every contact outside of Wales stimulated in him the energy to return to the major obsession of his life, rugby football. Thus it was no surprise to learn that the one time he stood for election as a Nationalist Candidate, on the eve of the ballot he sat at the house of a friend, discussing his recent appointment as British Lions coach while the loudspeakers blared his name and party outside, his own presence denied his supporters for the evening.

Carwyn brought a Welsh eye to rugby football, he was the most unbiased of men and moved so freely amongst rugby men everywhere because he so seldom put a Welsh point of view. When Dai Francis, the General Secretary of the Welsh Miners, presented miners' lamps to the Welsh members of his Lions team and over-enthusiastically stated that the Lions would have been nothing without the Welsh contingent, he got himself roundly ticked off by their coach who insisted the victory had been won by a British team from all four countries.

In the game, Carwyn's intelligence transcended nationality, as did many of his views, but at the same time he was inescapably Welsh and you could not know him for long without hearing him quote his favourite poet, Gwenallt, bidding you remember that you cannot care for the nations of the world unless first you learn to care for your own.

All of which did not matter much to the Italians, nor indeed, I suspect, to most of the teams he coached, but wherever he went he was in some senses a permanent extension of a National Cultural Museum. The moment I entered his flat in Rovigo, it was to be greeted by sizeable portraits of the Welsh language writers who mattered most to him – Gwenallt, Kate Roberts, Saunders Lewis. On one occasion, hotly engaged in an argument in which I was expressing the anti-nationalist view, he promptly stood up and obscured one of my own books with a volume of Gwynfor Evans, the Nationalist MP, adding impishly, 'You were saying?'

Yet, as I was to discover, in personal terms Carwyn's nationality was the least important fact about him. The man who so confidently asserted himself on public platforms, on the television screen and in the rugby dressing-rooms of the world, was a man who came crisply alive on specific occasions and then afterwards relapsed into a wayward self when he seemed at times incapable of looking after himself and was, moreover, not much interested in whatever consequences befell him. There were thus two Carwyn James personas – the public man and the private man. They were markedly different. Neither was false, but it was sometimes impossible to believe that the one belonged to the other.

I was soon shocked to see how badly affected he was by the virulent form of eczema which haunted him all the time I knew him. He had a habit of rubbing his hands together, a brisk and vigorous movement as if to convey immense enthusiasm at the slightest provocation.

'Another g and t, Richards?' he might say in his naval voice. We had both served in the Royal Navy.

'Plenty of tonic.'

One of my favourites amongst his many stories concerned the taciturn English rugby captain in the dressing-room at Twickenham who had heard that the Welsh were giving lengthy team talks and, when it was suggested that he might do the same, reluctantly agreed. But he was a man short on words and, having called for silence, cleared his throat uneasily.

'Right, gentlemen! Today we are playing the Welsh, ahem.' There was an awkward pause while he struggled for the next sentence.

'All I can say is, we've got to beat the bastards!' A further pause.

'Er … has anybody here got a fag?'

End of team talk.

Carwyn told this many times always grinding his palms together as he did so, and it wasn't long before I realised that the skin on his palms was unnaturally hardened by this constant rubbing. In fact, there was not a part of his body that was unaffected by the eczema apart from his face. In the privacy of his flat, he couldn't wait to remove his shoes and socks. As the night wore on, that first night and every night after that, you could often hear him scratching in his sleep through the bedroom wall. He was to have various treatments, in hospital and out of it, including acupuncture, but nothing worked for long, although he never complained and ignored his condition so successfully that it embarrassed his friends more than it did him. This stoicism was an unexpected trait and his indifference to himself was matched only by his indifference to all possessions, from overcoats to suitcases to cars, all of which he abandoned when it suited him. To this day, I'm sure there are suitcases belonging to him dotted all over the world. He was a man who walked away from things and set no value upon them at all. 'Possessions' was an ugly word in his vocabulary.

Although no medical expert, I began by attempting to bully him into taking more care of himself. Creams, lotions, powders littered the bathroom. More often than not, he forgot to apply them as if he had long since decided that he was the victim of an incurable condition. I urged cotton underclothes, air, light, vitamin C, the simple sensible things, but my concern bored him. There were things to do, people to visit, visitors to receive.

He had announced my arrival, making me a celebrity, and, as I soon found, a friend of Carwyn's was welcome anywhere. He had been installed in Rovigo for just under a month. His top-floor flat in the Via I Monti was just around the corner from the flat where the two South African forwards lived, the *stranieri* or foreign 'guest' players allowed by the Italian rugby authorities to each major club in order to further playing skills. They were his neighbours and friends, constant companions, and then there were the Rovigo team. The chairman, Franco Olivieri, had read of Carwyn and approached him through a previous *straniero*, Bernard Thomas, who had returned to play for Llanelli. The famous coach was already a minor deity and I was immediately accepted as part of his entourage. Carwyn was taking Italian lessons from Angelo Morello, a schoolmaster who lived around the corner, the most gentle of men who soon began to translate Carwyn's rugby articles for the local newspaper. I became *il companiato di rugby*.

It was like joining a potentate. Newly installed, I was assured by Franco Olivieri that my lack of Italian could be redressed by repeating *molto stupida*! whenever spoken to, a practice he himself found came naturally, as an ex-hooker like myself, and we shook hands on it in friendship. Indeed, friendship became the key note as we went from restaurant to restaurant and bar to bar, and once to a village nearby where a small rugby club had laid on a function to commemorate the death of their one international, a prop forward who had learned the game in Italy and then played at top level in France, returning home to have the local stadium named after him. In the little whitewashed tavern the local wine was produced in quantity. Carwyn and I sat bemused at the tributes and it suddenly dawned on me that I was in a rugby world as intense as any at home. Listening to the speeches of praise in memory of the fallen hero, I learned three more words of Italian – *aggressivo*, *generoso* and *combativo* – which gave me enough to be going on with. When Carwyn and I rose to sing the Welsh hymn, *Calon Lân*, there was tumultuous applause, before and after and the flashlights of cameras seemed only natural. Later that night we were in the cellar of a local property owner, inspecting his wine vats, and sat up so late talking rugby in broken English that his wife began to hurl abuse down the stairs. From that night on, transport, invitations, discount in leather goods stores, at the tailor's, and prize dishes in restaurants came our way like autumn leaves blowing down the Via I Monti itself. I had worked for Hollywood moguls and film stars and spied on showbiz extravagance, but these were the gifts of ordinary people, the whole town and, somehow, always more personal.

'It was,' I said, 'the Rugby High Life.'

'Why not?' Carwyn said.

from *Carwyn* (1983)

The Authors

Richard Burton (1925-84) film star, once described by his fellow Welsh actor Keith Baxter as 'a gifted and enthusiastic rugby player, with a reputation as a fearless and dirty player whose vindictiveness on the field could be boundless'.

Eddie Butler (b.1957) rugby pundit and broadcaster, capped sixteen time for Wales from Pontypool (1980-84).

W.J.Townsend Collins (1868-1952) 'Dromio' of the South Wales *Argus*, local historian of Newport and Monmouthshire.

Gerald Davies (b.1945) writer, journalist and wondrous wing-three-quarter for Wales (1966-78) and the British Lions (1968-71).

Lewis Davies (b.1967) born in Penrhiwtyn, Neath; editor, publisher and writer.

Richard Davies (b.1967) playwright and builder, once second-team player of the year for Bryncoch RFC.

Carwyn James (1929-83) rugby intellectual and inspirational coach of Llanelli and the 1971 Lions; capped twice for Wales in 1958.

Frank Keating (b.1937) author and *Guardian* sports columnist.

Terry McLean (1913-2004) supreme among New Zealand rugby writers, knighted for his sports journalism.

Rupert Moon (b.1968) Rupert St John Henry Barker Moon played scum-half for Llanelli and won twenty-four caps Welsh between 1993 and 2001.

John Morgan (1928-88) writer and broadcaster on politics, rugby and music.

John Reason (1927-2007) for many years the crusty but astute rugby critic of the *Daily Telegraph*.

Alun Richards (1929-2004) Pontypridd-born novelist, short-story writer and playwright.

Dai Smith (b.1945) cultural historian, broadcaster, and Chair of the Arts Council of Wales.

Dylan Thomas (1913-53) poet.

Gwyn Thomas (1913-81) writer, schoolteacher, broadcaster and humorist.

Alan Watkins (1933-2010) born in Ty-croes, Ammanford, political correspondent and rugby columnist.

Harri Webb (1920-94) librarian, nationalist, poet, and author of topical ballads and patriotic songs.

Gareth Williams (b.1945) historian and broadcaster. John Stuart Williams (1920-2001) poet and teacher.

Gareth Williams

Gareth Williams has written and broadcast extensively on the sporting and musical history of South Wales. His books include the prize-winning *Fields of Praise* (with Dai Smith), *1905 and All That*, *George Ewart Evans, Heart and Soul – the Character of Welsh Rugby* and *More Heart and Soul* (both co-edited with Huw Richards and Peter Stead), *Valleys of Song: Music and Society in Wales 1840-1914*, and *Sport*, an anthology of Welsh sports writing. His most recent book is *Wales and its Boxers – the Fighting Tradition* (co-edited with Peter Stead). He sings with the Pendyrus choir and is Emeritus Professor of History at the University of Glamorgan where he was Director of the Centre for Modern and Contemporary Wales.

Gerald Davies

Thomas Gerald Reames Davies was one of the most gifted of an outstanding generation of Welsh rugby players that brought lustre to the game and pleasure to millions in the 1970s. He won 46 caps between 1966 and 1978, captained Cambridge University, Cardiff and Wales, and toured with the British Lions to South Africa in 1968 and New Zealand in 1971. He was manager of the 2009 Lions in South Africa and is now Chairman of the British and Irish Lions and the WRU's representative on the International Rugby Board. An accomplished writer, his books include *Gerald – an autobiography* (1979), *Welsh Rugby Scrapbook* (1983) and *Sidesteps: A Rugby Diary 1984-5*, written with John Morgan. He has been writing for *The Times* since 1980 and in 2002 was awarded a CBE for services to sport and young people.